Z GRILLS

WOOD PELLET GRILL & SMOKER
COOKBOOK

HEALTHY, FAST & FRESH RECIPES FOR EVERYONE

AROUND THE WORLD

INDIRA ORTIZ

CONTENTS

INTRODUCTION

How the Z Grills Wood Pellet Grill Works

Pellet grills use all natural hardwood sawdust which is formed into little ¼ inch pieces as fuel. In the 1980s the popularity of using pellets in place of wood for household stoves was expanded to include grills. The burning pellets give your food a nice smoky flavor with consistent temperature.

Pellet grills work on the same principles as pellet stoves. Pellets are put into the hopper and the auger pushes the pellets from the hopper into the firepot to burn. On basic pellet grills the temperature cannot be adjusted, however on more sophisticated models, the temperature can be altered to suit the needs of the grill master. Pellet grills combine the best of both the grilling and smoking to produce the taste, texture, and appearance that you want when grilling meat, fish, vegetables or fruit. The infamous grill sear can also be achieved when using a cast iron grill grate or skillet preheated on the grill.

Pellet grills are much quicker to heat than traditional charcoal grills. While quick and easy, gas grills lack the taste and genuine flavor that pellet and charcoal grills provide and BBQ lovers insist upon.

What Makes the Z Grills Wood Pellet Grill Worthwhile?

1. For Baking and More

Pellet grills are worth the price for those who want to bake and use other cooking methods beyond grilling. Grilling is fine when you want to cook a few steaks or burgers, but if you want to get the most out of a grill, consider a pellet model. You can reach a high temperature that is perfect for baking cakes and other desserts or broiling corn and other vegetables for side dishes. These grills can also handle barbecue and other cooking methods too.

2. Less Expensive

Not only do pellet grills cost less upfront, but they also cost less over the long term. You can get a good wood pellet grill for half of what it would cost to buy a gas grill of the same size and with the same features. With gas grills, you need to keep an eye on your propane tank too.

With pellet grills, you can get a bag of wood pellets for around the same amount as a new tank costs. That bag will last longer though, which helps you save money. Pellet grills are more affordable than charcoal models too because a bag of wood pellets costs so much less than a bag of charcoal briquettes.

3. Other Reasons to Choose the Z Grills Pellet Grill

➤ Some of the other reasons why we think a pellet grill is worth the price include:

➤ You can better regulate and control the temperature of the grill

➤ Pellet grills give you the freedom to let your food cook as you do other tasks

➤ You don't need to deal with bulky and heavy propane tanks

➤ Most have a temperature setting that you can select, which will then maintain that temperature

➤ Pellet grills come in a range of prices for all budgets

➤ Many of the top pellet grills can last for a decade or longer

➤ You can easily experiment with different cooking methods and foods

➤ The grills are easy to clean after you finish cooking

Ten Tips for Using Your Z Grills Wood Pellet Grill

1. START EARLY: Many of the flavor compounds in smoke are fat and water soluble, which means that whatever you are cooking will absorb smoky flavors best when it is raw. As the surface cooks and dries out, the smoke does not penetrate as well.

2. GO LOW AND SLOW (MOST OF THE TIME): Real barbecue is cooked slowly over low, indirect heat—with wood smoke—because that's a traditional way to make sinewy meats so moist and tender that you hardly need teeth. But don't miss easy opportunities for adding sweet wood aromas to foods that are grilled over a hot fire for just minutes, like steaks, shrimp, and even vegetables.

3. REGULATE THE HEAT WITH A WATER PAN: Big fluctuations in smoking temperatures can tighten and dry out foods. Whenever you cook for longer than an hour with charcoal, use a pan of water to help stabilize the heat and add some humidity. Obviously a water smoker already has one, but for a charcoal grill, use a large disposable foil pan, and don't forget to refill it.

4. DON'T OVERDO IT. The biggest mistake rookies make is adding too much wood, chunk after chunk, to the point where the food tastes bitter. In general, you should smoke food for no longer than half its cooking time. Also, the smoke should flow like a gentle stream, not like it is billowing out of a train engine.

5. WHITE SMOKE IS GOOD; BLACK SMOKE IS BAD: Clean streams of whitish smoke can layer your food with the intoxicating scents of smoldering wood. But if your fire lacks enough ventilation, or your food is directly over the fire and the juices are burning, blackish smoke can taint your food or lead to unpleasant surprises when you lift the lid.

6. KEEP THE AIR MOVING: Keep the vents on your charcoal grill open and position the vent on the lid on the side opposite the coals. The open vents will draw smoke from the charcoal and wood below so that it swirls over your food and out the top properly, giving you the best ventilation and the cleanest smoke. If the fire gets too hot, close the top vent almost all the way.

7. DON'T GO GOLFING: Smoking is a relatively low-maintenance way of cooking—but remain mindful and be safe. Never leave a lit fire unattended, and check the temperature every hour or so. You might need to adjust the vents or add more charcoal.

8. TRY NOT TO PEEK: Every time you open a grill, you lose heat and smoke—two of the most important elements for making a great meal. Open the lid only when you really need to tend to the fire, the water pan, or the food. Ideally take care of them all at once—and quickly. Otherwise, relax and keep a lid on it.

9. LET THE BARK GET DARK: Barbecued meat should glisten with a dark mahogany crust that borders on black. This "bark" is the delicious consequence of fat and spices sizzling with smoke on the surface of the meat and developing a caramelized crust over the luscious meat below. Before you take the meat off the grill or wrap it in foil, make sure the bark is dark enough that it tastes like heaven.

10. FEATURE THE STAR ATTRACTION: The main ingredient in any smoked recipe is like the lead singer in a rock-and-roll band. Every other flavor should play a supporting role. In other words, don't upstage something inherently delicious with a potent marinade, heavy-handed seasonings, or thick coats of sauce. Harmonizing flavors in ways that feature the main ingredient is what separates the masters from the masses.

Deep Clean Methods for the Z Grills Wood Pellet Grill

1. Use an onion on a BBQ fork. The onion has acids that break down fat and the water inside the onion works like a steam cleaner. Rub-down the grates after cooking and scraping as usual and when the grates are still pretty warm. You can add some salt on the onion's scrubbing side to get better traction and scrubbing power. The onion can also be sliced thinner to reach between the grills.

Use the fork to angle under the grill edges to remove anything stuck underneath. You won't need to peel the onion, just slice it with the skin still on. After that, give a generous spray down with vinegar and water mix to wash away the onion build-up. This will further break down oils and fat that has dried onto the metal grill surfaces.

2. Caked on grills will need a strong cup of coffee. Brew up a batch of your favorite mud and put your grill into a washing tub. Pour the coffee over the grill until it's submerged. Let it sit until the natural acids in the coffee break down the fats and dried-on food. This can take 3 hours of soaking, so sit back and have a cup as well. Afterward, you can scrub off the grill with any scrubby sponge or pot cleaner.

This method is great for cleaning both sides of the grill and should be done at least once per season. It doesn't matter what kind of coffee you use, but the stronger you make it- the better. Arabica coffee is good to use, and it should be made from coffee grounds on a drip machine.

3. You can't beat the power of white vinegar and water at getting any grill sparkling clean. Put your grills in a plastic tub and fill it up with a 60/40 mix of vinegar and water. Let it sit for 5 minutes and then use a lemon to scrub-off the remaining caked-on grill grate. You could use nearly anything handy such an onion, lemon, or dried corn cobs. This method is especially strong to remove very gunked-up grates in a hurry.

Especially if you didn't have the time to clean your grill in a while! Not only is this method safe and chemical-free, but your metal also isn't getting scratched by using scraping tools. The left-over vinegar and water mix can simply be flushed without harm to the environment.

BAKING RECIPES

Rosemary Cranberry Apple Sage Stuffing

Servings: 7   Cooking Time: 45 Minutes

Ingredients:

- 10 Cups Day Old Diced Bread, Sliced Loaf
- 2 1/2 Cups Broth, Chicken
- 1 Cup Butter, Unsalted
- 1 Cup Diced Celery, Cut
- 1 1/2 Cups Fresh Cranberries
- 1 Beaten Egg
- 1 Medium Granny Smith Apple, Peel, Core And Dice
- 2 Tbsp Minced Parsley, Fresh
- 1 Tbsp Minced Rosemary, Fresh
- 2 Tbsp Roughly Chopped Sage
- Salt And Pepper
- 1 Tbsp Minced Thyme
- 2 Cups Diced Yellow Onion, Sliced

Directions:

1. Supply your smoker with wood pellets and follow the start-up procedure. Preheat the grill, with the lid closed, to 350° F.

2. Melt butter over medium heat. Add onions then celery and cook until onions start to become translucent.

3. In a large bowl, mix together bread, apples, cranberries, cooked onion and celery mixture, and fresh herbs.

4. Add half of the chicken broth to the mixture and stir.

5. Beat together eggs and the rest of the chicken broth in a small bowl. Pour into the bread mixture and stir until completely combined.

6. Add salt and pepper to taste.

7. Pour stuffing into a cast iron pan or baking dish. Cover with foil and bake on the grill for 30 minutes. Remove the foil and cook for an additional 15 minutes.

8. Serve immediately and enjoy!

Chocolate Almond Cake

Servings: 8

Cooking Time: 50 Minutes

Ingredients:

- 7 oz good quality dark chocolate; melted
- 5 eggs; separated
- Pinch salt
- 6.5 oz caster sugar
- 7 oz butter; cubed at room temperature
- 7 oz ground almonds
- 1 oz cocoa powder
- 1 tsp. baking powder
- Icing sugar; for dusting

Directions:

1. Supply your smoker with wood pellets and follow the start-up procedure. Preheat the grill, with the lid closed, to 347 °F.

2. Beat together the butter and sugar until light and fluffy. Then beat in the yolks, one at a time.

3. Gently fold in the almonds.

4. Add the melted chocolate and mix well.

5. Beat the egg whites with a pinch of salt in a separate bowl until stiff.

6. Sift the baking powder and cocoa powder into the cake mix and fold in gently, then fold in the egg whites.

7. Pour the mix into an 8.5" round spring form cake tin (greased and lined), smooth over, and bake in the center of the grill for about 50 minutes. If the top starts to dry out after 25-30 minutes, cover with foil.

Green Bean Casserole Circa 1955

Servings: 6

Cooking Time: 30 Minutes

Ingredients:

- ➤ 1 1/2 Pound Green Beans, fresh
- ➤ 1 Can cream of mushroom soup
- ➤ 1/2 Cup milk
- ➤ 2 Teaspoon soy sauce
- ➤ 1/2 Teaspoon Worcestershire sauce
- ➤ 1/2 Teaspoon black pepper
- ➤ 1.334 Cup French's Original Crispy Fried Onions
- ➤ 1/4 Cup red bell pepper, diced

Directions:

1. In a mixing bowl, combine the beans (trimmed and cooked until tender, or may use 2 16 oz. cans), soup, milk, soy sauce, Worcestershire sauce, black pepper, 2/3 cup of the onion rings, and red pepper, if using. Transfer to a 1-1/2 quart casserole dish.

2. Supply your smoker with wood pellets and follow the start-up procedure. Preheat the grill, with the lid closed, to 375° F.

3. Cook the casserole until the filling is hot and bubbling, 25 to 30 minutes. Top with the remaining onions and cook for 5 to 10 minutes more, or until the onions are crisp and beginning to brown. Grill: 375 °F

Quick Baked Dinner Rolls

Servings: 8

Cooking Time: 30 Minutes

Ingredients:

- 2 Tablespoon quick-rise yeast
- 1 Teaspoon salt
- 1/4 Cup sugar
- 3 1/3 Cup flour
- 1/4 Cup unsalted butter, softened
- 1 egg
- cooking spray
- 1 egg, for egg wash

Directions:

1. Combine yeast and warm water in a small bowl to activate the yeast. Let sit until foamy, about 5-10 minutes.

2. Combine salt, sugar, and flour in the bowl of a stand mixer fitted with the dough hook. Pour water and yeast into the dry ingredients with the machine running on low.

3. Add butter and egg and mix for 10 minutes gradually increasing the speed from low to high.

4. Form the dough into a ball and place in a buttered bowl. Cover with a cloth and let the dough rise for approximately 40 minutes.

5. Transfer the risen dough to a lightly floured surface and divide into 8 pieces forming a ball with each.

6. Lightly spray a cast iron pan with cooking spray and arrange balls in the pan. Cover with a cloth and let rise 20 minutes.

7. Supply your smoker with wood pellets and follow the start-up procedure. Preheat the grill, with the lid closed, to 375° F.

8. Brush rolls with egg wash and then bake for 30 minutes until lightly browned. Serve hot. Enjoy!

Grill: 375 ˚F

Easy Smoked Cornbread

Servings: 4

Cooking Time: 75 Minutes

Ingredients:

- ➤ 2 cups self rising flour
- ➤ 1 1/2 cups white corn meal
- ➤ 2 cups sharp cheddar cheese
- ➤ 1/2 cup sour cream
- ➤ 1/2 cup sugar
- ➤ 1 Tbsp baking powder
- ➤ 1 teaspoon sea salt
- ➤ 1 12 oz can of evaporated milk
- ➤ 1/2 cup vegetable oil
- ➤ 2 large eggs beaten

Directions:

1. Mix all ingredients together well and fold into a greased baking pan (such as a round cake Pan).

2. Supply your smoker with wood pellets and follow the start-up procedure. Preheat the grill, with the lid closed, to 375° F. Smoke on 375 °F for 1 hour and 15 minutes or until toothpick comes clean and edges look brown.

3. Rub some butter on top and sprinkle a little Fred's Butt Rub on top before serving.

4. Enjoy!

Chicken Pot Pie

Servings: 6

Cooking Time: 60 Minutes

Ingredients:

- ➢ 2 Chicken, Boneless/Skinless
- ➢ 1 Cream Of Chicken Soup, Can
- ➢ 1 Tsp Curry Powder
- ➢ 1/2 Cup Mayo
- ➢ 1 1/2 Cups Mixed Frozen Vegetables
- ➢ 1 Onion, Sliced
- ➢ 2 Frozen Pie Shell, Deep
- ➢ 1/2 Cup Sour Cream

Directions:

1. Supply your smoker with wood pellets and follow the start-up procedure. Preheat the grill, with the lid closed, to 425° F.

2. Cut the onion in half and place on the grates of the grill. If you"re using fresh chicken breasts, barbecue the chicken at the same time as the onions. The chicken is fully cooked when the internal temperature reached 170F. While the onion and chicken are cooking, prepare the pie crust by putting one crust in a pie plate. When the chicken and onions are done, shred chicken and chop onion into small pieces and place in the prepared pie plate along with the mixed vegetables.

3. Combine cream of chicken soup, mayo, sour cream, and curry powder in a bowl. Pour into the pie crust with the chicken and mix to combine. Wet the sides of the bottom crust with a small amount of water and top with the second pie crust. Push gently along the sides of the crust to seal the two pie crusts together.

4. Place in the and bake for 40 minutes, or until the crust is golden brown. Serve hot.

Cheese Mac

Servings: 6 - 10   Cooking Time: 60 Minutes

Ingredients:

- 5 Tbsp All-Purpose Flour
- 4 Strips Bacon
- Black Pepper
- 2 Cups Breadcrumbs
- 4 Oz Brie
- 4 Oz Brie Cheese
- ½ Cup Butter, Melted
- 12 Oz Cheddar Cheese, Grated
- 3 Cloves Garlic, Minced
- 2 Tbsp Extra Virgin Olive Oil
- 1 Tsp Fresh Grated Nutmeg
- 1 Tsp Ground Cayenne
- 8 Oz, Grated Gruyere Cheese
- 1 Cup Heavy Cream
- 1, Minced Jalapeno Pepper
- 4 Oz Mozzarella Cheese, Grated
- 2 Tbsp Parsley, Minced Fresh
- 12 Oz Raclette
- To Taste Salt
- 5 Tbsp Unsalted Butter
- 4 Oz Whole Milk, Warm
- 1 Yellow Onion, Diced

Directions:

1. Supply your smoker with wood pellets and follow the start-up procedure. Preheat the grill, with the lid closed, to 350° F. Bring a large saucepan of water to a boil. Add the pasta and cook according to the package instructions for al dente. Drain.

2. Heat the oil in a large saucepan over medium-high heat.

3. Add the onion and cook for about 5 minutes, stirring often, until lightly colored, then add the garlic and the jalapeño and cook for 2 more minutes.

4. Reduce the heat to medium, add the butter, and stir until melted. Add the flour and cook, stirring often, for 5 minutes to form a light roux.

5. Add the cheeses, the milk, and cream, reduce the heat to medium-low, and cook, stirring often, until the cheese is melted, and a smooth sauce comes together, about 7 minutes.

6. Stir in the cayenne and truffle oil, then add the pasta and stir to fully coat it in the sauce. Season with salt and pepper. Transfer the mixture to a 12-inch cast-iron skillet and cover with aluminum foil.

7. Place on the grill and bake for 20 minutes. Remove the foil and cover the mac and cheese with the breadcrumbs.

8. Return to the grill and bake for another 15 to 20 minutes, until the cheese is bubbling and the breadcrumbs are golden brown. Serve family style right out of the skillet.

Onion Cheese Nachos

Servings: 6

Cooking Time: 10 Minutes

Ingredients:

- ➢ 1 Pound Beef, Ground
- ➢ 3 Cups Cheddar Cheese, Shredded
- ➢ 1 Green Bell Pepper, Diced
- ➢ 1/2 Cup Green Onion
- ➢ 1/2 Cup Red Onion, Diced
- ➢ 1 Large Bag Tortilla Chip

Directions:

1. Supply your smoker with wood pellets and follow the start-up procedure. Preheat the grill, with the lid closed, to 350° F.

2. While you're waiting, empty a large bag of nacho chips evenly onto a cast iron pan. Start loading up with toppings - cooked ground beef, red onion, red pepper, cheese, green onions. These are just the toppings we had on hand, so feel free to add anything you like! Make sure you do a couple layers of chips so everyone gets a good serving of nachos. And don't be skimpy with the cheese - lay it on heavy!

3. Place your loaded nachos on the grill and let the hot smoke melt your toppings into one cheesy creation. Heat at 350°F for 10 minutes or until the cheese has fully melted. Remove and serve with sour-cream and salsa.

Spiced Lemon Cherry Pie

Servings: 6-8

Cooking Time: 60 Minutes

Ingredients:

- ➢ 1/2 Teaspoon Cinnamon, Ground
- ➢ 1/2 Teaspoon Cloves, Ground
- ➢ 1/2 Cup Cornstarch
- ➢ 1 Pound Frozen Sweet Dark Cherries, Thawed
- ➢ 1 Teaspoon Water (Beaten With Egg) 1 Egg
- ➢ 1 Lemon, Juice
- ➢ 1 Lemon, Zest
- ➢ 2 Prepared Store Bought Or Homemade Pie Crust
- ➢ 1 Teaspoon Hickory Honey Sea Salt Seasoning
- ➢ 1 Cup Sugar, Granulated
- ➢ 1 Teaspoon Vanilla Extract

Directions:

1. In a large bowl, mix together the thawed cherries and their juices, sugar, cornstarch, lemon zest, lemon juice, cinnamon, clove, vanilla extract and Hickory Honey Sea Salt. Allow to sit for 30 minutes.

2. Flour a work surface and roll out one of the prepared pie crusts so that it fits a 9 inch pie tin. Fill with the cherry pie filling and refrigerate. When the pie is chilled, roll out the second pie crust, brush the edge of the first pie crust with the egg mixture, top with the second pie crust, crimp the edge with a fork, and chill. Alternatively, cut the second pie crust into strips and form a lattice pattern, attaching the strips with the egg mixture. Chill the pie for 15-30 minutes, or until the dough is very cold and firm. Brush the top of the pie with the remaining egg mixture.

3. Supply your smoker with wood pellets and follow the start-up procedure. Preheat the grill, with the lid closed, to 350° F and grill for 45 minutes to 1 hour, or until the pie crust is golden and firm and the filling is bubbly. Remove from the grill and allow to cool at room temperature for at least 4 hours to set the filling, then serve and enjoy!

Baked Green Chile Mac & Cheese By Doug Scheiding

Servings: 8

Cooking Time: 120 Minutes

Ingredients:

- 24 Ounce shredded cheddar cheese, divided
- 8 Ounce mozzarella cheese, shredded
- 6 Tablespoon unsalted butter
- 16 Ounce large dry elbow macaroni noodles
- 2 1/2 Cup half-and-half
- 2 Cup heavy whipping cream
- 8 Ounce cream cheese
- 16 Ounce 505 Southwestern Hatch Valley Flame Roasted Green Chile
- 2 Tablespoon Prime Rib Rub

Directions:

1. Supply your smoker with wood pellets and follow the start-up procedure. Preheat the grill, with the lid closed, to 165° F.

2. Place 16 ounces of the shredded cheddar and the 8 ounces of shredded mozzarella cheese into a shallow pan or cookie sheet and place the pan directly on the grill grate. Smoke for 30 to 40 minutes. Remove from grill and set aside. Grill: 165 °F

3. Increase the grill temperature to 300°F and place a large disposable aluminum half pan in the Traeger with the butter. Remove the pan from the grill after the butter has fully melted. Grill: 300 °F

4. Add the noodles to the pan, along with half-and-half, heavy whipping cream, 16 ounces of the cold smoked cheddar, all of the smoked mozzarella cheese and cream cheese broken into small pieces. Add the green chiles to taste (12 ounces for mild and 16 ounces for spicy) and stir to combine.

5. Place the pan in the grill and bake for 2 hours, stirring every 20 minutes. If macaroni and cheese looks like it is getting dry, add a little more half-and-half and stir to combine. Grill: 300 °F

6. During the last 20 minutes of cooking, sprinkle the remaining (unsmoked) cheddar cheese on top and add a light dusting of Traeger Prime Rib Rub. Serve hot. Enjoy!

SEAFOOD RECIPES

Garlic Pepper Shrimp Pesto Bruschetta

Servings: 12

Cooking Time: 15 Minutes

Ingredients:

- 12 Slices Bread, Baguette
- 1/2 Tsp Chili Pepper Flakes
- 1/2 Tsp Garlic Powder
- 4 Cloves Garlic, Minced
- 2 Tbsp Olive Oil
- 1/2 Tsp Paprika, Smoked
- 1/4 Tsp Parsley, Leaves
- Pepper
- Pesto
- Salt
- 12 Shrimp, Jumbo

Directions:

1. Supply your smoker with wood pellets and follow the start-up procedure. Preheat the grill, with the lid closed, to 350° F. Place the baguette slices on a baking sheet lined with foil. Stir together the olive oil, and minced garlic, then brush both sides of the baguette slices with the mix. Place the pan inside the grill, and bake for about 10-15 minutes.

2. In a skillet, add a splash of olive oil, shrimp, chili powder, garlic powder, smoked paprika, salt pepper, and grill on medium-high heat for about 5 minutes (until the shrimp is pink). Be sure to stir often. Once pink, remove pan from heat. Once the baguettes are toasted, let them cool for 5 minutes, then spread a layer of pesto onto each one, then top with a shrimp, and serve.

Barbecued Shrimp

Servings: 4

Cooking Time: 10 Minutes

Ingredients:

- ➢ 1 pound peeled and deveined shrimp, with tails on
- ➢ 2 tablespoons olive oil
- ➢ 1 batch Dill Seafood Rub

Directions:

1. Soak wooden skewers in water for 30 minutes.
2. Supply your smoker with wood pellets and follow the start-up procedure. Preheat the grill, with the lid closed, to 375°F.
3. Thread 4 or 5 shrimp per skewer.
4. Coat the shrimp all over with olive oil and season each side of the skewers with the rub.
5. Place the skewers directly on the grill grate and grill the shrimp for 5 minutes per side. Remove the skewers from the grill and serve immediately.

Sweet Mandarin Salmon

Servings: 2

Cooking Time: 10 Minutes

Ingredients:

- ➢ 1 Whole lime juice
- ➢ 1 Teaspoon sesame oil
- ➢ 1 1/2 Cup Mandarin Orange Sauce
- ➢ 1 1/2 Tablespoon soy sauce
- ➢ 2 Tablespoon cilantro, finely chopped
- ➢ Freshly cracked black pepper
- ➢ 1 Whole (4 oz) wild salmon fillets

Directions:

1. Supply your smoker with wood pellets and follow the start-up procedure. Preheat the grill, with the lid closed, to 375° F.

2. For the glaze, combine Mandarin orange sauce, lime juice, sesame oil, soy sauce, cilantro and fresh cracked black pepper. Mix together.

3. Cut the salmon into 4 fillets. Brush with glaze and place directly on the grill grate, skin side down.

4. Cook until salmon reaches an internal temperature of 155 degrees F (about 15-20 minutes). Half way through cook time, brush salmon again with the glaze.

5. Remove the salmon from the grill and serve with remaining glaze if desired. Enjoy!

Shrimp Cabbage Tacos With Lime Cream

Servings: 4

Cooking Time: 10 Minutes

Ingredients:

- 1/4 Cabbage, Shredded
- 2 Tsp Cilantro, Chopped
- Corn Tortillas
- 1/2 Lime, Wedges
- 1/4 Cup Mayonnaise
- Blackened Sriracha Rub
- 1/4 Red Bell Pepper, Chopped
- 1 Lb Shrimp, Peeled & Deveined
- 1/4 Cup Sour Cream
- 2 Tsp Vegetable Oil
- 1/2 White Onion, Chopped

Directions:

1. Place shrimp In a medium bowl. Season with Blackened Sriracha Rub, then drizzle with vegetable oil. Toss by hand to coat well then set aside.

2. In a small mixing bowl, stir together mayonnaise, sour cream, and fresh lime juice. Season to taste with Blackened Sriracha. Set aside.

3. In a small mixing bowl, combine jalapeño, onion, red bell pepper, and cilantro. Set aside.

4. Supply your smoker with wood pellets and follow the start-up procedure. Preheat the grill, with the lid closed, till over medium heat. If using a grill, preheat a cast iron skillet over medium-heat.

5. Place tortillas on the griddle to warm each side, then turn off the burner below.

6. Transfer shrimp to the hot griddle, and cook for 4 to 6 minutes, tossing occasionally, until opaque. For spicier shrimp, season with additional Blackened Sriracha.

7. Assemble tacos: shredded cabbage, shrimp, pepper mixture, then drizzle with sauce. Serve warm with fresh lime wedges.

Summer Paella

<table>
<tr><td>Servings: 6</td><td>Cooking Time: 45 Minutes</td></tr>
</table>

Ingredients:

- 6 tablespoons extra-virgin olive oil, divided, plus more for drizzling
- 2 green or red bell peppers, cored, seeded, and diced
- 2 medium onions, diced
- 2 garlic cloves, slivered
- 1 (29-ounce) can tomato purée
- 1½ pounds chicken thighs
- Kosher salt
- 1½ pounds tail-on shrimp, peeled and deveined
- 1 cup dried thinly sliced chorizo sausage
- 1 tablespoon smoked paprika
- 1½ teaspoons saffron threads
- 2 quarts chicken broth
- 3½ cups white rice
- 2 (7½-ounce) cans chipotle chiles in adobo sauce
- 1½ pounds fresh clams, soaked in cold water for 15 to 20 minutes2 tablespoons chopped fresh parsley
- 2 lemons, cut into wedges, for serving

Directions:

1. Make the sofrito: On the stove top, in a saucepan over medium-low heat, combine ¼ cup of olive oil, the bell peppers, onions, and garlic, and cook for 5 minutes, or until the onions are translucent.

2. Stir in the tomato purée, reduce the heat to low, and simmer, stirring frequently, until most of the liquid has evaporated, about 30 minutes. Set aside. (Note: The sofrito can be made in advance and refrigerated.)

3. Supply your smoker with wood pellets and follow the start-up procedure. Preheat, with the lid closed, to 450°F.

4. Heat a large paella pan on the smoker and add the remaining 2 tablespoons of olive oil.

5. Add the chicken thighs, season lightly with salt, and brown for 6 to 10 minutes, then push to the outer edge of the pan.

6. Add the shrimp, season with salt, close the lid, and smoke for 3 minutes.

7. Add the sofrito, chorizo, paprika, and saffron, and stir together.

8. In a separate bowl, combine the chicken broth, uncooked rice, and 1 tablespoon of salt, stirring until well combined.

9. Add the broth-rice mixture to the paella pan, spreading it evenly over the other ingredients.

10. Close the lid and smoke for 5 minutes, then add the chipotle chiles and clams on top of the rice.

11. Close the lid and continue to smoke the paella for about 30 minutes, or until all of the liquid is absorbed.

12. Remove the pan from the grill, cover tightly with aluminum foil, and let rest off the heat for 5 minutes.

13. Drizzle with olive oil, sprinkle with the fresh parsley, and serve with the lemon wedges.

Grilled Tilapia With Blistered Cherry Tomatoes

Servings: 4   Cooking Time: 15 Minutes

Ingredients:

- 1½lb (680g) tilapia fillets or other mild white fish fillets
- chopped fresh curly or flat-leaf parsley
- for the marinade
- ½ cup extra virgin olive oil
- 1 garlic clove, peeled and smashed with a chef's knife
- 3 tbsp freshly squeezed lemon juice
- 1 tsp smoked paprika
- ½ tsp coarse salt
- ¼ tsp freshly ground black pepper
- for the tomatoes
- 2 tbsp extra virgin olive oil
- 2 pints (1 liter) cherry tomatoes (red, yellow, or heirloom varieties)
- coarse salt
- freshly ground black pepper

Directions:

1. Place a cast iron skillet on the grate. Supply your smoker with wood pellets and follow the start-up procedure. Preheat the grill, with the lid closed, to 400° F.

2. In a jar with a tight-fitting lid, make the marinade by combining the ingredients. Shake the jar vigorously to emulsify the ingredients.

3. Place the fillets in a single layer in a nonreactive baking dish. Pour half the marinade over them and turn the fillets to thoroughly coat. Cover with plastic wrap and refrigerate for 15 minutes. (Refrigerate no more than 30 minutes or the acid in the marinade will begin to cook the fish.)

4. Place the olive oil in the skillet. Add the tomatoes and season with salt and pepper. Stir to coat. Cook the tomatoes until they begin to blister and collapse, about 5 minutes, stirring once or twice. Remove the skillet from the grill and transfer the tomatoes to a bowl.

5. Carefully lift each fish fillet from the marinade and let the excess drip off. Place the fillets on the grate at a slight angle to the bars. Lightly season with salt and pepper. Grill until the fish flakes easily when pressed with a fork, about 4 to 5 minutes per side, turning carefully with a thin-bladed spatula.

6. Transfer the fillets to a warmed platter. Top with some of the tomatoes. (Place the remaining tomatoes in a serving bowl.) Scatter the parsley around the platter. Drizzle some of the remaining marinade over the top. Serve immediately.

Honey Balsamic Salmon

Servings: 2

Cooking Time: 25 Minutes

Ingredients:

- ➤ 1 Medium salmon fillet
- ➤ Fin & Feather Rub
- ➤ 1/2 Cup balsamic vinegar
- ➤ 1 Tablespoon minced garlic
- ➤ 2 Tablespoon honey

Directions:

1. Season the fillet with the Traeger Fin & Feather Rub.

2. Make the glaze: Combine the vinegar, garlic and honey in a small saucepan. Simmer over medium heat until reduced by half. Usually 10 to 15 minutes. The glaze will be properly reduced when it coats the back of a spoon. Using a basting brush, coat the fillet with the glaze.

3. Supply your smoker with wood pellets and follow the start-up procedure. Preheat the grill, with the lid closed, to 350° F.

4. Arrange the salmon fillet on the grill grate. Grill for 25 to 30 minutes, or until the salmon is opaque and flakes easily with a fork. Grill: 350 °F

5. Transfer to a platter or plates and serve immediately. If desired, heat any remaining glaze to a boil and drizzle over top of the salmon. Enjoy!

Bacon Wrapped Scallops

Servings: 8

Cooking Time: 20 Minutes

Ingredients:

- 24 jumbo deep sea diver scallops, dry-packed
- 1/2 Cup butter
- salt
- freshly ground black pepper
- 1 Clove garlic, minced
- 12 Slices thin-cut bacon, cut in half crosswise
- lemon wedges, for serving

Directions:

1. Remove the small, crescent-shaped muscle from the side of each scallop, if still attached. Dry the scallops thoroughly on paper towels, then transfer to a medium bowl.

2. Melt butter in a small saucepan, add garlic and cook for 1 minute. Let cool slightly then pour over the scallops. Season with salt and pepper and gently toss to coat.

3. Wrap a piece of bacon around each scallop and secure with a toothpick.

4. Supply your smoker with wood pellets and follow the start-up procedure. Preheat the grill, with the lid closed, to 400° F.

5. Arrange the scallops directly on the grill grate. Grill for 15 to 20 minutes, or until the scallop is opaque and the bacon has begun to crisp. If desired, you can turn the scallops on their side, bacon-side down, turning occasionally to crisp the bacon. Do not overcook. Grill: 400 ˚F

6. Transfer the scallops to a platter and serve with lemon wedges.

Bbq Oysters

Servings: 4

Cooking Time: 6 Minutes

Ingredients:

- 1 Pound unsalted butter, softened
- 1 Tablespoon Meat Church Holy Gospel BBQ Rub
- 1 Bunch green onions, chopped
- 2 Clove garlic, minced
- 12 oysters
- 1/4 Cup seasoned breadcrumbs
- 8 Ounce shredded pepper jack cheese
- Sweet & Heat BBQ Sauce
- 1/2 Bunch green onions, minced

Directions:

1. Supply your smoker with wood pellets and follow the start-up procedure. Preheat the grill, with the lid closed, to 375° F.

2. For the compound butter: Combine butter, garlic, onion and Meat Church Rub thoroughly.

3. Lay the butter on parchment paper or plastic wrap. Roll it up to form a log and tie each end with butcher's twine. Place in the freezer for an hour to solidify. You can use this butter on any grilled meat to enhance the flavor. You can also use a high-quality butter to replace the compound butter.

4. Shuck the oysters, keeping all of the juice in the shell. Sprinkle the oysters with breadcrumbs and place directly on the Traeger. Cook them for 5 minutes. You will be looking for the edge of the oyster to start to curl slightly.

5. After 5 minutes, place a spoonful of compound butter in the oysters. After the butter melts, add a pinch of pepper jack cheese.

6. Remove the oysters after 6 minutes on the grill total. Top oysters with a squirt of Traeger Sweet & Heat BBQ Sauce and a few chopped onions. Allow to cool for 5 minutes, then enjoy!

Smoked Mango Shrimp

Servings: 4

Cooking Time: 5 Minutes

Ingredients:

➢ 2 Tablespoon Olive Oil

➢ 1 Pound Raw Tail-On, Thawed And Deveined Shrimp, Uncooked

Directions:

1. Supply your smoker with wood pellets and follow the start-up procedure. Preheat the grill, with the lid closed, to 425° F. Rinse shrimp off in sink with cold water. Place in bowl and season generously with Mango Magic seasoning and olive oil. Toss well in bowl.

2. Thread several shrimp onto a skewer, so that they are all just touching each other. Repeat with other skewers and remaining shrimp.

3. Grill shrimp for 2 - 3 minutes on each side, or until pink and opaque all the way through. Remove from grill and serve immediately.

Dijon-smoked Halibut

Servings: 6

Cooking Time: 120 Minutes

Ingredients:

- 4 (6-ounce) halibut steaks
- ¼ cup extra-virgin olive oil
- 2 teaspoons kosher salt
- 1 teaspoon freshly ground black pepper
- ½ cup mayonnaise
- ½ cup sweet pickle relish
- ¼ cup finely chopped sweet onion
- ¼ cup chopped roasted red pepper
- ¼ cup finely chopped tomato
- ¼ cup finely chopped cucumber
- 2 tablespoons Dijon mustard
- 1 teaspoon minced garlic

Directions:

1. Rub the halibut steaks with the olive oil and season on both sides with the salt and pepper. Transfer to a plate, cover with plastic wrap, and refrigerate for 4 hours.

2. Supply your smoker with wood pellets and follow the start-up procedure. Preheat, with the lid closed, to 200°F.

3. Remove the halibut from the refrigerator and rub with the mayonnaise.

4. Put the fish directly on the grill grate, close the lid, and smoke for 2 hours, or until opaque and an instant-read thermometer inserted in the fish reads 140°F.

5. While the fish is smoking, combine the pickle relish, onion, roasted red pepper, tomato, cucumber, Dijon mustard, and garlic in a medium bowl. Refrigerate the mustard relish until ready to serve.

6. Serve the halibut steaks hot with the mustard relish.

PORK RECIPES

Wet-rubbed St. Louis Ribs

Servings: 2

Cooking Time: 240 Minutes

Ingredients:

- ➢ 1/2 Cup brown sugar
- ➢ 1 Tablespoon ground cumin
- ➢ 1 Tablespoon ancho chile powder
- ➢ 1 Tablespoon smoked paprika
- ➢ 1 Tablespoon garlic salt
- ➢ 3 Tablespoon balsamic vinegar
- ➢ 1 Rack St. Louis-style ribs
- ➢ 2 Cup apple juice

Directions:

1. In a bowl, combine all ingredients except ribs. Place wet rub on both sides of ribs; let sit for at least 10 minutes.

2. Supply your smoker with wood pellets and follow the start-up procedure. Preheat the grill, with the lid closed, to 180° F.

3. Turn temperature to 250°F; transfer the ribs into a foil pan, or wrap in tinfoil. Pour apple juice in the foil. Place foiled ribs back on grill. Cook for 2 hours. Remove from grill and let rest 10 minutes. Enjoy! Grill: 250 °F

3-2-1 Bbq Baby Back Ribs

Servings: 6   Cooking Time: 360 Minutes

Ingredients:

- 2 Rack baby back pork ribs
- 1/3 Cup yellow mustard
- 1/2 Cup apple juice, divided
- 1 Tablespoon Worcestershire sauce
- Pork & Poultry Rub
- 1/2 Cup dark brown sugar
- 1/3 Cup honey, warmed
- 1 Cup 'Que BBQ Sauce

Directions:

1. If your butcher has not already done so, remove the thin silverskin membrane from the bone-side of the ribs by working the tip of a butter knife or a screwdriver underneath the membrane over a middle bone. Use paper towels to get a firm grip, then tear the membrane off.

2. In a small bowl, combine the mustard, 1/4 cup of apple juice (reserve the rest) and the Worcestershire sauce. Spread the mixture thinly on both sides of the ribs and season with Traeger Pork & Poultry Rub.

3. Supply your smoker with wood pellets and follow the start-up procedure. Preheat the grill, with the lid closed, to 180° F.Smoke the ribs, meat-side up for 3 hours.

4. After the ribs have smoked for 3 hours, transfer them to a rimmed baking sheet and increase the grill temperature to 225℉.

5. Tear off four long sheets of heavy-duty aluminum foil. Top with a rack of ribs and pull up the sides to keep the liquid enclosed. Sprinkle half the brown sugar on the rack, then top with half the honey and half the remaining apple juice. Use a bit more apple juice if you want more tender ribs. Lay another piece of foil on top and tightly crimp the edges so there is no leakage. Repeat with the remaining rack of ribs.

6. Return the foiled ribs to the grill and cook for an additional 2 hours.

7. Carefully remove the foil from the ribs and brush the ribs on both sides with Traeger 'Que Sauce. Discard the foil. Arrange the ribs directly on the grill grate and continue to grill until the sauce tightens, 30 to 60 minutes more.

8. Let the ribs rest for a few minutes before serving. Enjoy!

Maple Syrup Bacon Wrapped Tenderloin

Servings: 5

Cooking Time: 30 Minutes

Ingredients:

- 1 Package Bacon, Thick Cut
- 1/4 Cup Maple Syrup
- 2 Tbsp Olive Oil
- 3 Tbsp Competition Smoked Rub
- 1 Trimmed With Silver Skin Removed Pork, Tenderloin

Directions:

1. Lay the strips of bacon out flat, with each strip slightly overlapping the other.

2. Sprinkle the pork tenderloin with 1 tablespoon of the Competition Smoked Rub and lay in the center.

3. Wrap with bacon over the tenderloin and tuck in the ends.

4. In a small bowl, mix the olive oil, maple syrup and remaining seasoning together and brush onto the wrapped tenderloin.

5. Supply your smoker with wood pellets and follow the start-up procedure. Preheat the grill, with the lid open, to 350° F.

6. When the grill is ready, place your tenderloin on the grill and cook, turning, for 15 minutes.

7. Increase the grill temperature to 400°F and grill for another 15 minutes or until the internal temperature is 145°F. Serve and enjoy!

Maple Baby Backs

Servings: 4-6

Cooking Time: 240 Minutes

Ingredients:

- 2 (2- or 3-pound) racks baby back ribs
- 2 tablespoons yellow mustard
- 1 batch Sweet Brown Sugar Rub
- ½ cup plus 2 tablespoons maple syrup, divided
- 2 tablespoons light brown sugar
- 1 cup Pepsi or other non-diet cola
- ¼ cup The Ultimate BBQ Sauce

Directions:

1. Supply your smoker with wood pellets and follow the start-up procedure. Preheat the grill, with the lid closed, to 180°F.

2. Remove the membrane from the backside of the ribs. This can be done by cutting just through the membrane in an X pattern and working a paper towel between the membrane and the ribs to pull it off.

3. Coat the ribs on both sides with mustard and season them with the rub. Using your hands, work the rub into the meat.

4. Place the ribs directly on the grill grate and smoke for 3 hours.

5. Remove the ribs from the grill and place them, bone-side up, on enough aluminum foil to wrap the ribs completely. Drizzle 2 tablespoons of maple syrup over the ribs and sprinkle them with 1 tablespoon of brown sugar. Flip the ribs and repeat the maple syrup and brown sugar application on the meat side.

6. Increase the grill's temperature to 300°F.

7. Fold in three sides of the foil around the ribs and add the cola. Fold in the last side, completely enclosing the ribs and liquid. Return the ribs to the grill and cook for 30 to 45 minutes.

8. Remove the ribs from the grill and unwrap them from the foil.

9. In a small bowl, stir together the barbecue sauce and remaining 6 tablespoons of maple syrup. Use this to baste the ribs. Return the ribs to the grill, without the foil, and cook for 15 minutes to caramelize the sauce.

10. Cut into individual ribs and serve immediately.

Baby Back Ribs With Mustard Slather

Servings: 4

Cooking Time: 120 Minutes

Ingredients:

- ➢ 2 racks of baby back ribs, each about 2lb (1kg)
- ➢ all-purpose barbecue rub
- ➢ low-carb barbecue sauce (optional)
- ➢ for the mustard
- ➢ ½ cup yellow or brown mustard
- ➢ 2 tbsp dill pickle juice or apple cider vinegar

Directions:

1. Supply your smoker with wood pellets and follow the start-up procedure. Preheat the grill, with the lid closed, to 325° F.

2. Remove the thick membrane on the bone side of the ribs. Don't remove the thin membrane on top of the bones because it holds them together. Trim off any odd bits of meat or excess fat. Place the ribs on a rimmed sheet pan.

3. In a small bowl, make the mustard slather by combining the mustard and pickle juice. Brush the ribs on both sides with the mixture and then season with the barbecue rub.

4. Place the ribs on the grate and smoke until the ribs are tender, about 1½ to 2 hours. (A toothpick inserted between bones should go in with little resistance. The meat will also have pulled back from the bone about ½ inch [1.25cm].) Brush the ribs with barbecue sauce (if using) during the last 10 minutes of smoking. Place the ribs meat side down on the grate for 5 minutes. Turn and grill for 5 minutes more. This sets the sauce.

5. Transfer the ribs to a cutting board. Use a sharp knife to cut the slabs in half or into individual ribs. Serve immediately with more barbecue sauce.

Old-fashioned Roasted Glazed Ham

Servings: 8

Cooking Time: 60 Minutes

Ingredients:

- ➢ 1 (10 lb) fully cooked bone-in spiral cut ham
- ➢ 1 Cup pineapple juice
- ➢ 1/2 Cup brown sugar
- ➢ 1 cinnamon stick
- ➢ 14 whole cloves
- ➢ 1 Whole Pineapple, fresh
- ➢ 10 Cherries, fresh, sweet

Directions:

1. Supply your smoker with wood pellets and follow the start-up procedure. Preheat the grill, with the lid closed, to 325° F.

2. Rinse ham under cold water and pat dry with paper towel.

3. In a saucepan combine pineapple juice, brown sugar, cinnamon stick and four cloves. Bring to a boil. Reduce heat to medium low and simmer for about 15 minutes or until pineapple juice is reduced by half, thick and syrupy.

4. Brush half of the glaze onto the ham and into the folds of the cut slices. Reserve the other half of the glaze for later.

5. Cut pineapple in desired sized pieces, about 2 inch squares, then place on ham with a cherry and a clove to pin in place, repeating all over ham.

6. Put ham in a deep baking dish with fat side up. Place on the Traeger and cook for about 1-¼ hours. Grill: 325 ˚F

7. Carefully remove from Traeger and brush remaining glaze onto ham.

8. Return ham to Traeger and continue cooking for another 15 to 20 minutes, until internal temperature of ham reaches 160°F. Grill: 325 ˚F Probe: 160 ˚F

9. Allow ham to rest for 15 – 20 minutes before serving. Enjoy!

Smoked Bbq Ribs

Servings: 4

Cooking Time: 300 Minutes

Ingredients:

- 2 Rack St. Louis-style ribs
- 1/4 Cup Big Game Rub
- 1 Cup apple juice
- BBQ Sauce

Directions:

1. Pat ribs dry and peel the membrane from the back of the ribs.

2. Apply an even coat of rub to the front, back and sides of the ribs. Let sit for 20 minutes and up to 4 hours if refrigerated.

3. Supply your smoker with wood pellets and follow the start-up procedure. Preheat the grill, with the lid closed, to 225° F.

4. Place ribs, bone side down on grill. Put apple juice in a spray bottle and spray the ribs after 1 hour of cooking. Spray every 45 minutes thereafter. Grill: 225 °F Probe: 201 °F

5. After 4-1/2 hours, check the internal temperature of ribs. Ribs are done when internal temperature reaches 201°F. If not, check back in another 30 minutes. Grill: 225 °F Probe: 201 °F

6. Once ribs are done, brush a light layer of your favorite Traeger BBQ Sauce on the front and back of the ribs. Let the sauce set for 10 minutes. After the sauce has set, take ribs off the grill and let rest for 10 minutes. Slice ribs in between the bones and serve with extra sauce. Enjoy!

Grilled Raspberry Chipotle Pork Ribs

Servings: 4

Cooking Time: 180 Minutes

Ingredients:

➢ Baby Back Rib

➢ Original Bbq Sauce

➢ Raspberry Chipotle Spice Rub

Directions:

1. Begin by gently rinsing off your ribs in cool water. Pat dry and remove the flavor blocker (thin membrane on the underside of the ribs) to allow the seasoning to permeate right into the meat.

2. Generously season your ribs with Raspberry Chipotle seasoning and place in the refrigerator for an hour for flavor to set in.

3. Supply your smoker with wood pellets and follow the start-up procedure. Preheat the grill, with the lid open, to 250° F. Place your seasoned rack of ribs on the grill and let cook for 2 hours. Next, lather on a thick coating of Original BBQ Sauce, turn up the grill to 300°F and let your ribs roast for another hour. Remove, cut and serve for a meal that will surely make its way into the weekly rotation.

Bbq Pork Belly

Servings: 6

Cooking Time: 180 Minutes

Ingredients:

- ➤ 1 (3 lb) pork belly, skin removed
- ➤ 4 Tablespoon salt
- ➤ 1/2 Teaspoon black pepper
- ➤ Pork & Poultry Rub

Directions:

1. Supply your smoker with wood pellets and follow the start-up procedure. Preheat the grill, with the lid closed, to 275° F.

2. Meanwhile, season pork belly on both sides with salt, pepper and Traeger Pork & Poultry Rub. Place pork belly directly on the grill grate and cook for 3 to 3-1/2 hours or until the internal temperature reaches 200°F. Grill: 275 °F Probe: 200 °F

3. Remove from grill and let rest 10 to 15 minutes before slicing.

4. Serve in tacos, mac and cheese, nachos or your favorite dish. Enjoy!

Bbq Pulled Pork With Sweet & Heat Bbq Sauce

Servings: 4

Cooking Time: 540 Minutes

Ingredients:

- 10 Pound Bone-In Pork Butt
- 2 Tablespoon Pork & Poultry Rub
- 1 1/2 Cup apple juice
- 4 Tablespoon brown sugar
- 1 Tablespoon salt
- 1 To Taste salt
- 1 To Taste Pork & Poultry Rub
- 1 As Needed Sweet & Heat BBQ Sauce

Directions:

1. Trim pork butt of all excess fat leaving 1/4" of the fat cap attached. Combine 2 Tbsp Pork and Poultry rub, apple juice, brown sugar, and salt in a small bowl stirring until most of the sugar and salt are dissolved. Inject the pork butt every square inch or so with the apple juice mixture. Season the exterior of the pork butt with remaining rub.

2. Supply your smoker with wood pellets and follow the start-up procedure. Preheat the grill, with the lid closed, to 225° F.

3. Place pork butt directly on the grill grate and cook for about 6 hours or until the internal temperature reaches 160℉. Grill: 225 ℉ Probe: 160 ℉

4. Wrap the pork butt in two layers of foil and pour in 1/2 cup of apple juice. Secure tin foil tightly to contain the apple juice. Increase temperature to 275℉ and return to grill in a pan large enough to hold the pork butt in case of leaks. Cook an additional 3 hours or until internal temperature reaches 205℉. Grill: 275 ℉ Probe: 205 ℉

5. Remove from the grill and discard the bone. Shred the pork removing any excess fat or tendons. Season with additional Pork and Poultry Rub and salt if needed.

6. Add Sweet & Heat BBQ sauce and serve. Enjoy!

Pretzel Bun With Pulled Pork

Servings: 4

Cooking Time: 300 Minutes

Ingredients:

- ⅓ Cup Apple Cider Vinegar
- 1 ½ Cups Bbq Sauce, Divided
- 1 Qt. Chicken Stock
- ⅓ Cup Ketchup
- 3 Tbsp Pulled Pork Rub, Divided
- 1, 4 Lb. Pork Shoulder, Bone In
- 4 Pretzel Buns

Directions:

1. Supply your smoker with wood pellets and follow the start-up procedure. Preheat the grill, with the lid open, to 400° F. If using a gas or charcoal grill, set it up for medium-high heat. In a bowl, combine the apple cider vinegar, chicken stock, ketchup, and 1 tablespoon of Pulled Pork Rub. Whisk well to combine and set aside.

2. Season the pork shoulder with the remaining 2 tablespoons of Pulled Pork Seasoning on all sides of the pork shoulder, then place on the grill and sear on all sides until golden brown, about 10 minutes.

3. Remove the pork shoulder from the grill and place in the disposable aluminum pan. Pour the sauce over the pork shoulder. It should come about 1/3 to ½ way up the side of the pork shoulder. Cover the top of the pan tightly with aluminum foil.

4. Reduce the temperature of your grill to 250°F. Place the foil pan on the grill and cook for 4 to 5 hours, or until the pork is tender and falling off the bone.

5. Remove the pork from the grill and allow to rest for 15 minutes. Drain the liquid from the pan, reserving about a cup, then shred the pork and cover with the reserved liquid. Set 3 ½ to 4 cups of pulled pork aside for sandwiches, and save the remaining for future use.

6. While pork is resting, place 1 cup of BBQ sauce in a skillet and heat to simmer. Toss in reserved shredded pork. Divide pork among 4 pretzel buns, spoon additional BBQ sauce over the top and dig in!

Rub-injected Pork Shoulder

Servings: 8-12

Cooking Time: 1200 Minutes

Ingredients:

➢ 1 (6- to 8-pound) bone-in pork shoulder

➢ 2 cups Tea Injectable made with Pork Rub

➢ 2 tablespoons yellow mustard

➢ 1 batch Pork Rub

Directions:

1. Supply your smoker with wood pellets and follow the start-up procedure. Preheat the grill, with the lid closed, to 225°F.

2. Inject the pork shoulder throughout with the tea injectable.

3. Coat the pork shoulder all over with mustard and season it with the rub. Using your hands, work the rub into the meat.

4. Place the shoulder directly on the grill grate and smoke until its internal temperature reaches 160°F and a dark bark has formed on the exterior.

5. Pull the shoulder from the grill and wrap it completely in aluminum foil or butcher paper.

6. Increase the grill's temperature to 350°F.

7. Return the pork shoulder to the grill and cook until its internal temperature reaches 195°F.

8. Pull the shoulder from the grill and place it in a cooler. Cover the cooler and let the pork rest for 1 or 2 hours.

9. Remove the pork shoulder from the cooler and unwrap it. Remove the shoulder bone and pull the pork apart using just your fingers. Serve immediately.

VEGETABLES RECIPES

Grilled Street Corn

Servings: 6

Cooking Time: 10 Minutes

Ingredients:

- 6 ears corn, husked
- 1 As Needed extra-virgin olive oil
- 1/4 Cup mayonnaise
- 1 Tablespoon ancho or guajillo chile powder
- 1/2 Cup chopped cilantro, plus more for serving
- 1 lime, zested and juiced
- salt
- 1/2 Cup Cotija cheese
- 1 As Needed cilantro, finely chopped

Directions:

1. Supply your smoker with wood pellets and follow the start-up procedure. Preheat the grill, with the lid closed, to 450° F.

2. Brush corn with oil and place on grill, turning occasionally.

3. While corn is on the grill, mix mayonnaise with chile powder, cilantro, lime juice and zest in a bowl. Season with salt.

4. After about 10 minutes corn should be cooked through and slightly charred on the outside. Remove from grill.

5. Top corn with chile mayonnaise then sprinkle on the Cotija cheese and chopped cilantro. Enjoy!

Grilled Asparagus & Honey-glazed Carrots

Servings: 4

Cooking Time: 35 Minutes

Ingredients:

- 1 Bunch asparagus, woody ends removed
- 1 Pound Carrots, peeled
- 2 Tablespoon olive oil
- sea salt
- 2 Tablespoon honey
- lemon zest

Directions:

1. Rinse all vegetables under cold water. Drizzle asparagus with olive oil and a generous sprinkling of sea salt. Generously drizzle carrots with honey and lightly sprinkle with sea salt.

2. Supply your smoker with wood pellets and follow the start-up procedure. Preheat the grill, with the lid closed, to 350° F.

3. Place carrots on the grill first and cook for 10-15 minutes, then add asparagus and cook both for another 15 to 20 minutes, or until they're done to your liking. Grill: 350 ˚F

4. Top the asparagus with some fresh lemon zest. Enjoy!

Roasted Vegetable Napoleon

Servings: 4

Cooking Time: 30 Minutes

Ingredients:

- ➢ 2 Whole sweet potatoes
- ➢ 2 Whole zucchini
- ➢ 2 Whole Squash
- ➢ 1 Whole red onion
- ➢ 2 Whole Bell Pepper, Red
- ➢ salt and pepper

Directions:

1. Supply your smoker with wood pellets and follow the start-up procedure. Preheat the grill, with the lid closed, to High heat.

2. Salt and pepper all vegetables and grill them on both sides. Begin with the peppers and onions as they will take a little longer to cook. Grill: 450 ˚F

Traeger Grilled Whole Corn

Servings: 4

Cooking Time: 25 Minutes

Ingredients:

- 3 green onions
- 6 Tablespoon butter, softened
- 1 Teaspoon chile powder
- 1 Teaspoon toasted sesame seeds
- 4 ears corn, in husk

Directions:

1. Supply your smoker with wood pellets and follow the start-up procedure. Preheat the grill, with the lid closed, to 325° F.

2. Place green onions directly on the grill grate and cook 15 minutes until lightly charred. Remove from grill and set aside.

3. Sesame-Chile Butter: Take butter out of fridge and let soften. Chop up charred green onions and add to butter along with chile powder and sesame seeds. Mash all ingredients together.

4. Grill corn, rotating occasionally, until husks are blackened (some will flake and fall off) and kernels are tender with some browned and charred spots, about 25 to 35 minutes. Grill: 325 °F

5. Let corn cool slightly, then shuck. Serve with the Sesame-Chile Butter. Enjoy

Broccoli-cauliflower Salad

Servings: 4

Cooking Time: 25 Minutes

Ingredients:

- 1½ cups mayonnaise
- ½ cup sour cream
- ¼ cup sugar
- 1 bunch broccoli, cut into small pieces
- 1 head cauliflower, cut into small pieces
- 1 small red onion, chopped
- 6 slices bacon, cooked and crumbled (precooked bacon works well)
- 1 cup shredded Cheddar cheese

Directions:

1. In a small bowl, whisk together the mayonnaise, sour cream, and sugar to make a dressing.
2. In a large bowl, combine the broccoli, cauliflower, onion, bacon, and Cheddar cheese.
3. Pour the dressing over the vegetable mixture and toss well to coat.
4. Serve the salad chilled.

Baked Breakfast Mini Quiches

Servings: 8

Cooking Time: 15 Minutes

Ingredients:

➢ cooking spray

➢ 1 Tablespoon extra-virgin olive oil

➢ 1/2 yellow onion, diced

➢ 3 Cup Spinach, fresh

➢ 10 eggs

➢ 4 Ounce shredded cheddar, mozzarella or Swiss cheese

➢ 1/4 Cup fresh basil

➢ 1 Teaspoon kosher salt

➢ 1/2 Teaspoon black pepper

Directions:

1. Spray a 12-cup muffin tin generously with cooking spray.

2. In a small skillet over medium heat, warm the oil. Add the onion and cook, stirring frequently, until softened, about 7 minutes. Add the spinach and cook until wilted, about 1 minute longer.

3. Transfer to a cutting board to cool, then chop the mixture so the spinach if broken up a little.

4. Supply your smoker with wood pellets and follow the start-up procedure. Preheat the grill, with the lid closed, to 350° F.

5. In a large bowl, whisk the eggs until frothy. Add the cooled onions and spinach, cheese, basil, 1 tsp salt and 1/2 tsp pepper. Stir to combine. Divide egg mixture evenly among the muffin cups.

6. Place tray on the grill and bake until the eggs have puffed up, are set, and are beginning to brown, about 18 to 20 minutes. Grill: 350 ˚F

7. Serve immediately, or allow to cool on a wire rack, then refrigerate in an air tight container for up to 4 days. Enjoy!

Baked Loaded Tater Tots

Servings: 6

Cooking Time: 35 Minutes

Ingredients:

- 2 Pound frozen tater tots
- 1 Can Black Beans
- 1 1/2 Cup leftover chili
- 1 Cup leftover queso
- 1 red onion, finely diced
- 1/2 Cup chopped cilantro
- 1/2 Cup sour cream
- 1 jalapeños, sliced

Directions:

1. Supply your smoker with wood pellets and follow the start-up procedure. Preheat the grill, with the lid closed, to 375° F.
2. Spread frozen tots out on a sheet tray and place directly on the grill grate.
3. Cook for 20 to 25 minutes or until tots are crispy. Grill: 375 ˚F
4. Top with warmed chili, queso and beans. Place back on the grill for 15 minutes. Grill: 375 ˚F
5. Remove from grill and top with red onion, cilantro, sour cream and jalapeño. Enjoy!

Roasted Sweet Potato Steak Fries

Servings: 4

Cooking Time: 40 Minutes

Ingredients:

- ➢ 3 Whole sweet potatoes
- ➢ 4 Tablespoon extra-virgin olive oil
- ➢ salt and pepper
- ➢ 2 Tablespoon fresh chopped rosemary

Directions:

1. Supply your smoker with wood pellets and follow the start-up procedure. Preheat the grill, with the lid closed, to 450° F.

2. Cut sweet potatoes into wedges and toss with olive oil, salt, pepper and rosemary. Spread on a parchment lined baking sheet and put in the grill. Cook for 15 minutes then flip and continue to cook until lightly browned and cooked through, about 40 to 45 minutes total. Grill: 450 °F

3. Serve with your favorite dipping sauce. Enjoy! Grill: 450 °F

Roasted Pumpkin Seeds

Servings: 8

Cooking Time: 40 Minutes

Ingredients:

➢ 1 Whole Pumpkin, seeds

➢ olive oil or vegetable oil

➢ Jacobsen Salt Co. Pure Kosher Sea Salt

Directions:

1. As soon as possible after removing the seeds from the pumpkin, rinse pumpkin seeds under cold water in a colander and pick out the pulp and strings.

2. Place the pumpkin seeds in a single layer on an oiled baking sheet, stirring to coat. Supply your smoker with wood pellets and follow the start-up procedure. Preheat the grill, with the lid closed, to 180° F.

3. Place the baking sheet with the seeds on the grill grate, close the lid, and smoke for 20 minutes. Grill: 180 ˚F

4. Sprinkle your seeds with salt and turn the temperature on your grill up to 325˚F. Roast the seeds until toasted, about 20 minutes. Check and stir seeds after the first 10 minutes. Grill: 325 ˚F

5. Seeds will be brown because they were smoked before being roasted. Enjoy!

Baked Artichoke Parmesan Mushrooms

Servings: 8

Cooking Time: 30 Minutes

Ingredients:

- 8 Cremini Mushroom Caps
- 6 1/2 Ounce artichoke hearts
- 1/3 Cup Parmesan cheese, grated
- 1/4 Cup mayonnaise
- 1/2 Teaspoon garlic salt
- your favorite hot sauce
- paprika

Directions:

1. Clean the mushrooms with a damp paper towel. Remove the stems and discard or save for another use.

2. Using a small spoon, scoop out the inside (gills, etc.). Combine the artichoke hearts, parmesan, mayonnaise, garlic salt, and hot sauce and mix well.

3. Mound the filling in the mushroom caps. Dust the tops with paprika.

4. Arrange the mushrooms in an oven-safe baking dish.

5. Supply your smoker with wood pellets and follow the start-up procedure. Preheat the grill, with the lid closed, to 350° F.

6. Bake the mushrooms (uncovered) until the filling is bubbling and just beginning to brown, about 25 to 30 minutes. Serve immediately. Grill: 350 ˚F

7. For a simple variation, stuff the mushrooms with your favorite bulk sausage and bake on your Traeger as directed above. Enjoy!

Grilled Chili-lime Corn

Servings: 8

Cooking Time: 45 Minutes

Ingredients:

- 12 Corn, ears
- 1 Teaspoon chili powder
- 1/2 Teaspoon onion powder
- 1 Teaspoon Leinenkugel's Summer Shandy Rub
- 2 lime, juiced
- 1 Tablespoon lime zest

Directions:

1. Soak the ears of corn, still in their husk, in water for 4 to 8 hours.

2. Supply your smoker with wood pellets and follow the start-up procedure. Preheat the grill, with the lid closed, to 350° F.

3. Place corn directly on grill grates. Turn corn every 15 minutes for 45 minutes total cooking time. Grill: 350 ℉

4. Combine chili powder, onion powder, Summer Shandy rub, lime juice, lime zest and butter in an oven safe dish and place in grill for 10 minutes. Remove corn and butter from the grill.

5. Pull corn husk back, but not off and remove corn silk. Using the corn husk as a handle, brush the corn with the melted chili-lime butter. Enjoy!

Grilled Asparagus And Spinach Salad

Servings: 8

Cooking Time: 10 Minutes

Ingredients:

- 4 Fluid Ounce apple cider vinegar
- 8 Fluid Ounce Honey Bourbon BBQ Sauce
- 2 Bunch asparagus, ends trimmed
- 3 Fluid Ounce extra-virgin olive oil
- 2 Ounce Beef Rub
- 24 Ounce Spinach, fresh
- 4 Ounce candied pecans
- 4 Ounce feta cheese

Directions:

1. Combine apple cider vinegar and Traeger Apricot BBQ Sauce to create salad dressing.
2. Supply your smoker with wood pellets and follow the start-up procedure. Preheat the grill, with the lid closed, to High heat.
3. Toss the asparagus with Olive Oil and the Beef Shake. Put asparagus in the Traeger Grilling Basket and move the basket to the grill grate.
4. Grill for about 10 minutes. Remove the asparagus once it is cooked. Grill: 350 ˚F
5. Place the hot asparagus right on top of the bowl of spinach.
6. Add candied pecans, feta cheese & salad dressing then toss and serve. Enjoy!

POULTRY RECIPES

Jalapeño- & Cheese-stuffed Chicken

Servings: 4

Cooking Time: 30 Minutes

Ingredients:

- ➤ 4 boneless, skinless chicken breasts, each about 6 to 8oz (170 to 225g)
- ➤ 8 strips of thin-sliced bacon
- ➤ for the filling
- ➤ 4oz (110g) light cream cheese, at room temperature
- ➤ ⅓ cup shredded pepper Jack or Cheddar cheese
- ➤ 2 jalapeños, destemmed, deseeded, and minced
- ➤ 2 tbsp reduced-fat mayo
- ➤ 1 tsp chili powder
- ➤ ½ tsp coarse salt

Directions:

1. Supply your smoker with wood pellets and follow the start-up procedure. Preheat the grill, with the lid closed, to 375° F.

2. In a large bowl, make the filling by combining the ingredients. Mix well.

3. Use a sharp, thin-bladed knife to cut a deep pocket in the side of each chicken breast, angling the knife toward the opposite side. (Don't cut all the way through.) Spoon ¼ of the cheese filling into the pocket of each breast and gently press the edges of the pocket together to enclose. Wrap 2 slices of bacon in a spiral pattern around each breast.

4. Place the chicken on the grate at an angle to the bars. Grill until the chicken is cooked through, the filling melts, and the bacon is golden brown, about 25 to 30 minutes.

5. Transfer the pockets to a platter. Let rest for 2 minutes before serving.

Grilled Cheesy Chicken

Servings: 4

Cooking Time: 45 Minutes

Ingredients:

➢ 4 Aged Chedder Cheese, Sliced

➢ 32 Oz Chicken Broth

➢ 1 Tsp Extra-Virgin Olive Oil

➢ Sweet Heat Rub And Grill

➢ 4 Plump Chicken, Boneless/Skinless

Directions:

1. Supply your smoker with wood pellets and follow the start-up procedure. Preheat the grill, with the lid open, to 350° F.

2. Remove the chicken from the brine. Pat the breasts dry and lightly brush olive oil on both sides of the chicken. Take your knife and slice diagonally across the top of each breast. Sprinkle a lit amount of Sweet Heat Rub and Grill on each side.

3. Barbecue your chicken breasts for 30 minutes. Next, place a slice of cheddar cheese on top of each breast.

4. Heat for another 5-10 minutes or until the cheese has fully melted into the incisions you made earlier. Remove and serve for a tender chicken breast with a spicy kick and hot cheesy center. You'll receive too much credit for a recipe this easy.

Buffalo Chicken Wraps

Servings: 4

Cooking Time: 20 Minutes

Ingredients:

- ➢ 2 teaspoons poultry seasoning
- ➢ 1 teaspoon freshly ground black pepper
- ➢ 1 teaspoon garlic powder
- ➢ 1 to 1½ pounds chicken tenders
- ➢ 4 tablespoons (½ stick) unsalted butter, melted
- ➢ ½ cup hot sauce (such as Frank's RedHot)
- ➢ 4 (10-inch) flour tortillas
- ➢ 1 cup shredded lettuce
- ➢ ½ cup diced tomato
- ➢ ½ cup diced celery
- ➢ ½ cup diced red onion
- ➢ ½ cup shredded Cheddar cheese
- ➢ ¼ cup blue cheese crumbles
- ➢ ¼ cup prepared ranch dressing
- ➢ 2 tablespoons sliced pickled jalapeño peppers (optional)

Directions:

1. Supply your smoker with wood pellets and follow the start-up procedure. Preheat, with the lid closed, to 350°F.

2. In a small bowl, stir together the poultry seasoning, pepper, and garlic powder to create an all-purpose rub, and season the chicken tenders with it.

3. Arrange the tenders directly on the grill, close the lid, and smoke for 20 minutes, or until a meat thermometer inserted in the thickest part of the meat reads 170°F.

4. In another bowl, stir together the melted butter and hot sauce and coat the smoked chicken with it.

5. To serve, heat the tortillas on the grill for less than a minute on each side and place on a plate.

6. Top each tortilla with some of the lettuce, tomato, celery, red onion, Cheddar cheese, blue cheese crumbles, ranch dressing, and jalapeños (if using).

7. Divide the chicken among the tortillas, close up securely, and serve.

Smoked Thanksgiving Turkey

Servings: 6 - 8

Cooking Time: 300 Minutes

Ingredients:

- 1 Turkey Brining Kits
- 12 – 14 Lbs Turkey
- 1 Gallon Water, Cold
- 4 Cups + 1 Gallon Water, Warm

Directions:

1. Start by defrosting the turkey overnight in the refrigerator.

2. Once turkey has been defrosted begin to make the brine by adding 4 cups of water and the brine mixture to a large stockpot.

3. Bring the mixture to a boil and add 1 gallon of cold water.

4. Place the turkey in the brine bag and pour the brine mixture over the turkey and refrigerate 1 hour per pound.

5. Once turkey has been brined rinse the turkey with cold water and set on a pan.

6. Using the seasoning in the brine box, season the turkey. Once turkey has been seasoned, supply your smoker with wood pellets and follow the start-up procedure. Preheat the grill, with the lid closed, to 275° F.

7. Place your turkey in the smoker and place the temperature probe in the deepest part of the breast. Cook at 275 until the breast and thigh meat internal temperature has reached 165°F to 170°F.

8. Remove the turkey from the smoker, let cool, and cut the turkey into your desired pieces. Enjoy!

Hot Turkey Sandwich With Gravy

Servings: 4

Cooking Time: 10 Minutes

Ingredients:

➢ 8 Slices Bread, Sliced

➢ 1 Cup Gravy, Prepared

➢ 2 Cups Leftover Turkey, Shredded

Directions:

1. Supply your smoker with wood pellets and follow the start-up procedure. Preheat the grill, with the lid closed, to 400° F.

2. Place the BBQ Grill Mat on the grates of your preheated grill and lay the shredded turkey evenly across the mat to reheat for about 10 minutes.

3. Prepare or reheat the gravy. You"ll want to have the gravy warmed and ready as soon as the turkey is reheated and the bread is toasted.

4. Hold each slice of bread over the flame broiler to toast to your liking.

5. When all of your ingredients are hot, scoop 1/2 cup of the shredded turkey onto a piece of bread, generously cover with gravy and top with another piece of toasted bread. Serve immediately.

Grilled Chipotle Chicken Skewers

Servings: 4

Cooking Time: 25 Minutes

Ingredients:

- BBQ Sauce
- 1 cup spicy BBQ sauce
- 3 chipotle peppers
- 1 Tbsp adobo sauce
- Skewers
- Olive oil
- 2 lbs boneless skinless chicken breasts
- 10 thick-cut bacon strips
- 1 large green bell pepper, cut into 3/4 to 1 inch pieces
- 1 medium red onion, peeled and cut into 3/4 to 1 inch pieces
- Bamboo skewers
- Garnish: freshly chopped garnish

Directions:

1. Supply your smoker with wood pellets and follow the start-up procedure. Preheat the grill, with the lid closed.

2. Soak the wooden skewers in water for at least 10 to 15 minutes before skewering to avoid them burning as much.

3. Add all ingredients for the sauce to a blender. Blend until they are combined well.

4. Cut chicken into 3/4-inch bite-sized pieces. Cut bacon into 3/4-inch strips.

5. Thread bacon (folding the bacon in half before skewering), chicken, peppers, and onion onto the skewers, alternating as you go.

6. Arrange the skewers on the grill grate and cook for 10 minutes, turning every few minutes. Baste the skewers with BBQ sauce on all sides. Continue to baste and turn the skewers every minute or so to caramelize.

7. The chicken is cooked through when it reaches an internal temperature of 165 °F. The bacon should be nice and crispy at this point.

8. Remove the skewers from the grill and sprinkle with freshly chopped parsley.

Easy Bbq Chicken Wings

Servings: 4

Cooking Time: 40 Minutes

Ingredients:

- ➢ 1 Pack Chicken Wings
- ➢ Extra Virgin Olive Oil
- ➢ Champion Chicken Seasoning

Directions:

1. Supply your smoker with wood pellets and follow the start-up procedure. Preheat the grill, with the lid closed, to 350° F.
2. Blot the defrosted chicken wings dry with paper towels.
3. Brush oil onto each side of the wings and sprinkle with seasoning.
4. Grill at 350° for 40 minutes or until wings are crispy. Flip halfway through. Serve hot.

Baked Garlic Parmesan Wings

Servings: 4

Cooking Time: 40 Minutes

Ingredients:

- ➤ 3 1/2 Tablespoon Chicken Rub
- ➤ 5 Pound chicken wings
- ➤ 1 Cup butter
- ➤ 10 Clove garlic, minced
- ➤ 1/2 Cup unsalted butter
- ➤ 10 Clove garlic, finely diced
- ➤ 1 Cup shredded Parmesan cheese
- ➤ 3 Tablespoon chopped parsley

Directions:

1. Supply your smoker with wood pellets and follow the start-up procedure. Preheat the grill, with the lid closed, to 450° F.

2. In a large bowl, toss the wings with the Traeger Chicken Rub.

3. Place wings directly on the grill grate and cook for 20 minutes. Flip wings and cook for an additional 20 minutes. Grill: 450 ℉

4. Check the internal temperature of the wings, finished desired temperature is 165℉ to 180℉. Grill: 450 ℉ Probe: 165 ℉

5. To make the Garlic Sauce: While the chicken is cooking, combine butter, garlic and remaining rub in a medium sized saucepan and cook over medium heat on a stove top. Cook sauce for 8 to 10 minutes, stirring occasionally.

6. When wings are finished cooking, remove from grill and place in a large bowl. Toss wings with the garlic sauce, Parmesan cheese and parsley. Enjoy!

Turkey & Bacon Kebabs With Ranch-style Dressing

Servings: 8   Cooking Time: 25 Minutes

Ingredients:

- 1½lb (680g) skinless turkey tenders or boneless, skinless turkey breasts, cut into 1-inch (2.5cm) chunks
- 8 strips of thick-cut bacon
- 12 fresh bay leaves (optional)
- for the dressing
- 1 cup reduced-fat mayo
- 1 cup light sour cream
- ½ cup buttermilk or whole milk, plus more
- 2 tbsp minced fresh parsley
- 2 tbsp minced fresh chives
- 1 tbsp minced fresh dill
- 2 tsp freshly squeezed lemon juice
- 1 tsp Worcestershire sauce
- 1 tsp garlic salt
- 1 tsp onion powder
- ½ tsp coarse salt, plus more
- ½ tsp freshly ground black pepper, plus more

Directions:

1. In a large bowl, make the dressing by whisking together the mayo, sour cream, and buttermilk until smooth. Whisk in the remaining ingredients. Pour half the mixture into a small bowl. Cover and refrigerate.

2. Add the turkey to the mixture remaining in the bowl and toss to coat thoroughly. If the dressing seems too thick (dip-like), add more buttermilk 1 tablespoon at a time. Cover and refrigerate for 2 to 4 hours.

3. Supply your smoker with wood pellets and follow the start-up procedure. Preheat the grill, with the lid closed, to 375° F.

4. Place the bacon on the grate and cook until some of the fat has rendered and the bacon begins to brown, about 15 minutes. Remove the bacon from the grill to cool. Cut the bacon into 1-inch (2.5cm) squares. Set aside.

5. Drain the tenders and discard any excess dressing. Alternate threading the turkey, bacon pieces, and 3 bay leaves on a bamboo skewer. Repeat the threading with 3 more skewers.

6. Place the kebabs on the grate and grill until the turkey is cooked through, about 4 to 5 minutes per side, turning as needed.

7. Transfer the skewers to a platter. Serve with the reserved dressing.

Bourbon Chicken Waffles

Servings: 8 | Cooking Time: 30 Minutes

Ingredients:

- 1 Shot Of Bourbon
- 3 Cups Bread Crumbs
- 4 Horizontally Half Sliced Boneless, Skinless Chicken Breast
- Butter Flavored Cooking Spray
- 3 Eggs
- 1 Tsp Garlic Powder
- 1 Tsp Paprika, Powder
- Red Velvet Cake Mix
- 16 Oz. Reduced Fat Sour Cream
- Sweet Rib Rub
- ¼ Cup Vegetable Oil
- 1 ¼ Cup Water
- 1 Tbsp Worcestershire Sauce

Directions:

1. Supply your smoker with wood pellets and follow the start-up procedure. Preheat the grill, with the lid closed, to 350° F. If you're using a gas or charcoal grill, set up the grill for medium heat.

2. In a large bowl, combine the sour cream, bourbon, Worcestershire sauce, paprika, garlic powder, and Sweet Rib Rub seasoning. Add the chicken, turn the chicken breasts to coat, and cover the bowl. Refrigerate for 4-12 hrs.

3. Remove the chicken from the refrigerator and drain the marinade from the chicken. Mix together 3 cups bread crumbs and 2 tbsp Sweet Rib Rub. Mix the coating together and bread the chicken breasts.

4. Moisten a paper towel with cooking oil and using a pair of tongs, lightly grease the grill rack.

5. Grill or smoke until the internal temperature of the chicken reaches 170°F and the chicken is crispy and golden brown.

6. While the chicken is cooking, mix the eggs, vegetable oil, water, and red velvet cake mix in a bowl with the electric mixer.

7. Add the mix into the waffle iron and cook. Make as many waffles as the mix allows.

8. On a plate, place the cooked chicken on top of the waffles and top with maple syrup or honey.

Traeger Bbq Half Chickens

Servings: 2

Cooking Time: 60 Minutes

Ingredients:

- ➢ 1 (3 to 3-1/2 lb) fresh young chicken
- ➢ Leinenkugel's Summer Shandy Rub
- ➢ Apricot BBQ Sauce

Directions:

1. Place the chicken breast side down, on a cutting board with the neck pointing away from you. Cut along one side of the backbone, staying as close to the bone as possible, from the neck to the tail. Repeat on the other side of the backbone then remove it.

2. Open the chicken and slice through the white cartilage at the tip of the breastbone to pop it open. Cut down either side of the breast bone then use your fingers to pull it out. Flip the chicken over so it is skin side up and cut down the center splitting the chicken in half. Tuck the wings back on each chicken half.

3. Season on both sides with Traeger Leinenkugel's Summer Shandy Rub.

4. Supply your smoker with wood pellets and follow the start-up procedure. Preheat the grill, with the lid closed, to 375° F.

5. Place chicken directly on the grill grate skin side up and cook until the internal temperature reaches 160°F, about 60-90 minutes. Grill: 375 °F Probe: 160 °F

6. Brush the BBQ sauce all over the chicken skin and cook for an additional 10 minutes. Remove from grill and let rest 5 minutes before serving. Enjoy! Grill: 375 °F

Bbq Turkey Drumsticks

Servings: 6

Cooking Time: 120 Minutes

Ingredients:

- ➢ 1/2 Tbsp Black Pepper
- ➢ 1 Tbsp Brown Sugar
- ➢ 1/2 Tsp Cayenne Pepper
- ➢ 1/2 Tbsp Coriander, Ground
- ➢ 1/2 Tbsp Granulated Garlic
- ➢ 1 Package, Approx 4 Lbs Honeysuckle White® Turkey Drumsticks
- ➢ 1 Tbsp Kosher Salt
- ➢ 2 Tbsp Olive Oil

Directions:

1. Supply your smoker with wood pellets and follow the start-up procedure. Preheat the grill, with the lid open, to 225° F. If using a gas or charcoal grill, set it up for low, indirect heat.
2. Place Honeysuckle White® Turkey Legs on a sheet tray, coat with olive oil, then season with a blend of salt pepper, cayenne, brown sugar, granulated garlic, and ground coriander.
3. Place turkey legs in the smoking cabinet and smoke for 1 ½ hours, checking the internal temperature after 1 hour.
4. Increase the temperature to 325°F, transfer the turkey legs to the bottom grill grate and cook for another 25 to 30 minutes, until the internal temperature reaches 170°F.
5. Remove turkey drumsticks from the grill, allow to rest for 10 minutes, then serve warm.

APPETIZERS AND SNACKS

Pigs In A Blanket

Servings: 4-6

Cooking Time: 15 Minutes

Ingredients:

- ➢ 2 Tablespoon Poppy Seeds
- ➢ 1 Tablespoon Dried Minced Onion
- ➢ 2 Teaspoon garlic, minced
- ➢ 2 Tablespoon Sesame Seeds
- ➢ 1 Teaspoon salt
- ➢ 8 Ounce Original Crescent Dough
- ➢ 1/4 Cup Dijon mustard
- ➢ 1 Large egg, beaten

Directions:

1. When ready to cook, start your smoker at 350 degrees F, and preheat with lid closed, 10 to 15 minutes.

2. Mix together poppy seeds, dried minced onion, dried minced garlic, salt and sesame seeds. Set aside.

3. Cut each triangle of crescent roll dough into thirds lengthwise, making 3 small strips from each roll.

4. Brush the dough strips lightly with Dijon mustard. Put the mini hot dogs on 1 end of the dough and roll up.

5. Arrange them, seam side down, on a greased baking pan. Brush with egg wash and sprinkle with seasoning mixture.

6. Bake in smoker until golden brown, about 12 to 15 minutes.

7. Serve with mustard or dipping sauce of your choice. Enjoy!

Smoked Cashews

Servings: 6

Cooking Time: 60 Minutes

Ingredients:

➤ 1 pound roasted, salted cashews

Directions:

1. Supply your smoker with wood pellets and follow the start-up procedure. Preheat the grill, with the lid closed, to 120°F.

2. Pour the cashews onto a rimmed baking sheet and smoke for 1 hour, stirring once about halfway through the smoking time.

3. Remove the cashews from the grill, let cool, and store in an airtight container for as long as you can resist.

Smoked Cheese

Servings: 4

Cooking Time: 150 Minutes

Ingredients:

➢ 1 (2-pound) block medium Cheddar cheese, or your favorite cheese, quartered lengthwise

Directions:

1. Supply your smoker with wood pellets and follow the start-up procedure. Preheat the grill, with the lid closed, to 90°F.

2. Place the cheese directly on the grill grate and smoke for 2 hours, 30 minutes, checking frequently to be sure it's not melting. If the cheese begins to melt, try flipping it. If that doesn't help, remove it from the grill and refrigerate for about 1 hour and then return it to the cold smoker.

3. Remove the cheese, place it in a zip-top bag, and refrigerate overnight.

4. Slice the cheese and serve with crackers, or grate it and use for making a smoked mac and cheese.

Delicious Deviled Crab Appetizer

Servings: 30

Cooking Time: 10 Minutes

Ingredients:

➢ Nonstick cooking spray, oil, or butter, for greasing

➢ 1 cup panko breadcrumbs, divided

➢ 1 cup canned corn, drained

➢ ½ cup chopped scallions, divided

➢ ½ red bell pepper, finely chopped

➢ 16 ounces jumbo lump crabmeat

➢ ¾ cup mayonnaise, divided

➢ 1 egg, beaten

➢ 1 teaspoon salt

➢ 1 teaspoon freshly ground black pepper

➢ 2 teaspoons cayenne pepper, divided

➢ Juice of 1 lemon

Directions:

1. Supply your smoker with wood pellets and follow the start-up procedure. Preheat, with the lid closed, to 425°F.

2. Spray three 12-cup mini muffin pans with cooking spray and divide ½ cup of the panko between 30 of the muffin cups, pressing into the bottoms and up the sides. (Work in batches, if necessary, depending on the number of pans you have.)

3. In a medium bowl, combine the corn, ¼ cup of scallions, the bell pepper, crabmeat, half of the mayonnaise, the egg, salt, pepper, and 1 teaspoon of cayenne pepper.

4. Gently fold in the remaining ½ cup of breadcrumbs and divide the mixture between the prepared mini muffin cups.

5. Place the pans on the grill grate, close the lid, and smoke for 10 minutes, or until golden brown.

6. In a small bowl, combine the lemon juice and the remaining mayonnaise, scallions, and cayenne pepper to make a sauce.

7. Brush the tops of the mini crab cakes with the sauce and serve hot.

Chicken Wings With Teriyaki Glaze

Servings: 4   Cooking Time: 50 Minutes

Ingredients:

- 16 large chicken wings, about 3lb (1.4kg) total
- 1 to 1½ tbsp toasted sesame oil
- for the glaze
- ½ cup light soy sauce or tamari
- ¼ cup sake or sugar-free dark-colored soda
- ¼ cup light brown sugar or low-carb substitute
- 2 tbsp mirin or 1 tbsp honey

- 1 garlic clove, peeled, minced or grated
- 2 tsp minced fresh ginger
- 1 tsp cornstarch mixed with 1 tbsp distilled water (optional)
- for serving
- 1 tbsp toasted sesame seeds
- 2 scallions, trimmed, white and green parts sliced sharply diagonally

Directions:

1. Supply your smoker with wood pellets and follow the start-up procedure. Preheat the grill, with the lid closed, to 350° F.

2. Place the chicken wings in a large bowl, add the sesame oil, and turn the wings to coat thoroughly.

3. Place the wings on the grate at an angle to the bars. Grill for 20 minutes and then turn. Continue to cook until the wings are nicely browned and the meat is no longer pink at the bone, about 20 minutes more.

4. To make the glaze, in a saucepan on the stovetop over medium-high heat, combine the ingredients and bring the mixture to a boil. Reduce the glaze by 1/3, about 6 to 8 minutes. If you prefer your glaze to be glossy and thick, add the cornstarch and water mixture to the glaze and cook until it coats the back of a spoon, about 1 to 2 minutes more.

5. Transfer the wings to an aluminum foil roasting pan. Pour the glaze over them, turning to coat thoroughly. Place the pan on the grate and cook the wings until the glaze sets, about 5 to 10 minutes.

6. Transfer the wings to a platter. Scatter the sesame seeds and scallions over the top. Serve with plenty of napkins.

Jalapeño Poppers With Chipotle Sour Cream

Servings: 8   Cooking Time: 45 Minutes

Ingredients:

- 3 strips of thin-sliced bacon
- 12 large jalapeños, red, green, or a mix
- 8oz (225g) light cream cheese, at room temperature
- 1 cup shredded pepper Jack, Monterey Jack, or Cheddar cheese
- 1 tsp chili powder
- ½ tsp garlic salt
- smoked paprika
- for the sour cream
- 1¼ cups light sour cream
- juice of ½ lime
- ½ to 1 canned chipotle peppers in adobo sauce, finely minced, plus 1 tsp of sauce, plus more
- 1 tbsp minced fresh cilantro leaves
- ½ tsp coarse salt, plus more

Directions:

1. Supply your smoker with wood pellets and follow the start-up procedure. Preheat the grill, with the lid closed, to 375° F.

2. Line a rimmed sheet pan with aluminum foil and place a wire rack on top. Place the bacon in a single layer on the wire rack. Place the pan on the grate and grill until the bacon is crisp and golden brown, about 20 minutes. Transfer the bacon to paper towels to cool and then crumble. Set aside.

3. In a small bowl, make the chipotle sour cream by whisking together the ingredients. Add more salt, chipotle peppers, or adobe sauce to taste. Cover and refrigerate.

4. Slice the jalapeños lengthwise through their stems. Scrape out the veins and seeds with the edge of a small metal spoon.

5. In a small bowl, beat together the cream cheese, shredded cheese, chili powder, and garlic salt. Stir in the crumbled bacon. Mound the cream cheese mixture in the jalapeño halves. Line another rimmed sheet pan with aluminum foil and place a wire rack on top. Place the jalapeños filled side up in a single layer on the wire rack.

6. Place the sheet pan on the grate and roast the jalapeños until the filling has melted and the peppers have softened, about 20 to 25 minutes. (They should no longer look bright in color.) Remove the pan from the grill and let the peppers rest for 5 minutes.

7. Transfer the poppers to a platter and lightly dust with paprika. Serve with the chipotle sour cream.

Pulled Pork Loaded Nachos

Servings: 4   Cooking Time: 10 Minutes

Ingredients:

- 2 cups leftover smoked pulled pork
- 1 small sweet onion, diced
- 1 medium tomato, diced
- 1 jalapeño pepper, seeded and diced
- 1 garlic clove, minced
- 1 teaspoon salt
- 1 teaspoon freshly ground black pepper
- 1 bag tortilla chips
- 1 cup shredded Cheddar cheese
- ½ cup The Ultimate BBQ Sauce, divided
- ½ cup shredded jalapeño Monterey Jack cheese
- Juice of ½ lime
- 1 avocado, halved, pitted, and sliced
- 2 tablespoons sour cream
- 1 tablespoon chopped fresh cilantro

Directions:

1. Supply your smoker with wood pellets and follow the start-up procedure. Preheat, with the lid closed, to 375°F.

2. Heat the pulled pork in the microwave.

3. In a medium bowl, combine the onion, tomato, jalapeño, garlic, salt, and pepper, and set aside.

4. Arrange half of the tortilla chips in a large cast iron skillet. Spread half of the warmed pork on top and cover with the Cheddar cheese. Top with half of the onion-jalapeño mixture, then drizzle with ¼ cup of barbecue sauce.

5. Layer on the remaining tortilla chips, then the remaining pork and the Monterey Jack cheese. Top with the remaining onion-jalapeño mixture and drizzle with the remaining ¼ cup of barbecue sauce.

6. Place the skillet on the grill, close the lid, and smoke for about 10 minutes, or until the cheese is melted and bubbly. (Watch to make sure your chips don't burn!)

7. Squeeze the lime juice over the nachos, top with the avocado slices and sour cream, and garnish with the cilantro before serving hot.

Chorizo Queso Fundido

Servings: 4-6

Cooking Time: 20 Minutes

Ingredients:

- 1 poblano chile
- 1 cup chopped queso quesadilla or queso Oaxaca
- 1 cup shredded Monterey Jack cheese
- ¼ cup milk
- 1 tablespoon all-purpose flour
- 2 (4-ounce) links Mexican chorizo sausage, casings removed
- ⅓ cup beer
- 1 tablespoon unsalted butter
- 1 small red onion, chopped
- ½ cup whole kernel corn
- 2 serrano chiles or jalapeño peppers, stemmed, seeded, and coarsely chopped
- 1 tablespoon minced garlic
- 1 tablespoon freshly squeezed lime juice
- 1 teaspoon ground cumin
- 1 teaspoon salt
- 1 teaspoon freshly ground black pepper
- 1 tablespoon chopped fresh cilantro
- 1 tablespoon chopped scallions
- Tortilla chips, for serving

Directions:

1. Supply your smoker with wood pellets and follow the start-up procedure. Preheat, with the lid closed, to 350°F.
2. On the smoker or over medium-high heat on the stove top, place the poblano directly on the grate (or burner) to char for 1 to 2 minutes, turning as needed. Remove from heat and place in a closed-up lunch-size paper bag for 2 minutes to sweat and further loosen the skin.
3. Remove the skin and coarsely chop the poblano, removing the seeds; set aside.
4. In a bowl, combine the queso quesadilla, Monterey Jack, milk, and flour; set aside.
5. On the stove top, in a cast iron skillet over medium heat, cook and crumble the chorizo for about 2 minutes.
6. Transfer the cooked chorizo to a small, grill-safe pan and place over indirect heat on the smoker.
7. Place the cast iron skillet on the preheated grill grate. Pour in the beer and simmer for a few minutes, loosening and stirring in any remaining sausage bits from the pan.
8. Add the butter to the pan, then add the cheese mixture a little at a time, stirring constantly.
9. When the cheese is smooth, stir in the onion, corn, serrano chiles, garlic, lime juice, cuvmin, salt, and pepper. Stir in the reserved chopped charred poblano.
10. Close the lid and smoke for 15 to 20 minutes to infuse the queso with smoke flavor and further cook the vegetables.
11. When the cheese is bubbly, top with the chorizo mixture and garnish with the cilantro and scallions.
12. Serve the chorizo queso fundido hot with tortilla chips.

Chuckwagon Beef Jerky

Servings: 6   Cooking Time: 300 Minutes

Ingredients:

- 2½lb (1.2kg) boneless top or bottom round steak, sirloin tip, flank steak, or venison
- 1 cup sugar-free dark-colored soda
- 1 cup cold brewed coffee
- ½ cup light soy sauce
- ¼ cup Worcestershire sauce
- 2 tbsp whiskey (optional)
- 2 tsp chili powder
- 1½ tsp garlic salt
- 1 tsp onion powder
- 1 tsp pink curing salt

Directions:

1. Slice the meat into ¼-inch-thick (.5cm) strips, trimming off any visible fat or gristle. (Slice against the grain for more tender jerky and with the grain for chewier jerky.) Place the meat in a large resealable plastic bag.

2. In a small bowl, whisk together the soda, coffee, soy sauce, Worcestershire sauce, whiskey (if using), chili powder, garlic salt, onion powder, and curing salt (if using). Whisk until the salt dissolves. Pour the mixture over the meat and reseal the bag. Refrigerate for 24 to 48 hours, turning the bag several times to redistribute the brine.

3. Supply your smoker with wood pellets and follow the start-up procedure. Preheat the grill, with the lid closed, to 150° F.

4. Drain the meat and discard the brine. Place the strips of meat in a single layer on paper towels and blot any excess moisture.

5. Place the meat in a single layer on the grate and smoke for 4 to 5 hours, turning once or twice. (If you're aware of hot spots on your grate, rotate the strips so they smoke evenly.) To test for doneness, bend one or two pieces in the middle. They should be dry but still somewhat pliant. Or simply eat a piece to see if it's done to your liking.

6. For the best texture, when you remove the meat from the grill, place the still-warm jerky in a resealable plastic bag and let rest for 30 minutes. (You might see condensation form on the inside of the bag, but the moisture will be reabsorbed by the meat.) Or let the meat cool completely and then store in a resealable plastic bag or covered container. The jerky will last a few days at room temperature but will last longer (up to 2 weeks) if refrigerated.

Bayou Wings With Cajun Rémoulade

Servings: 8   Cooking Time: 40 Minutes

Ingredients:

- 16 large whole chicken wings or 32 drumettes and flats, about 3lb (1.4kg) total
- for the rub
- 1 tbsp kosher salt
- 1 tsp freshly ground black pepper
- 1 tsp paprika
- ½ tsp ground cayenne, plus more
- ½ tsp garlic powder
- ½ tsp celery salt
- ½ tsp dried thyme
- 2 tbsp vegetable oil
- for the rémoulade
- 1¼ cups reduced-fat mayo
- ¼ cup Creole-style or whole grain mustard
- 2 tbsp horseradish
- 2 tbsp pickle relish
- 1 tbsp freshly squeezed lemon juice
- 1 tsp paprika, plus more
- 1 tsp hot sauce, plus more
- 1 tsp Worcestershire sauce
- coarse salt
- for serving
- lemon wedges
- pickled okra (optional)

Directions:

1. Supply your smoker with wood pellets and follow the start-up procedure. Preheat the grill, with the lid closed, to 350° F.

2. If using whole wings, cut through the two joints, separating them into drumettes, flats, and wing tips. (Discard the wing tips or save them for chicken stock.) Alternatively, leave the wings whole. Place the chicken in a resealable plastic bag.

3. In a small bowl, make the rub by combining the ingredients. Mix well. Pour the rub over the wings and toss them to thoroughly coat. Refrigerate for 2 hours.

4. In a small bowl, make the Cajun rémoulade by whisking together the mayo, mustard, horseradish, pickle relish, lemon juice, paprika, hot sauce, and Worcestershire. Season with salt to taste. The mixture should be highly seasoned. Transfer to a serving bowl and lightly dust with paprika. Cover and refrigerate until ready to serve.

5. Remove the wings from the refrigerator and allow the excess marinade to drip off. Place the wings on the grate at an angle to the bars. Grill for 20 minutes and then turn. (They'll brown more evenly but will also have less of a tendency to stick.) Continue to cook until the wings are nicely browned and the meat is no longer pink at the bone, about 20 minutes more.

6. Remove the wings from the grill and pile them on a platter. Serve with the Cajun rémoulade, lemon wedges, and pickled okra (if using).

Roasted Red Pepper Dip

Servings: 8   Cooking Time: 45 Minutes

Ingredients:

- 4 red bell peppers, halved, destemmed, and deseeded
- 1 cup English walnuts, divided
- 1 small white onion, peeled and coarsely chopped
- 2 garlic cloves, peeled and smashed with a chef's knife
- ¼ cup extra virgin olive oil, plus more
- 1 tbsp balsamic vinegar or balsamic glaze
- 1 tsp honey (eliminate if using balsamic glaze)
- 1 tsp coarse salt, plus more
- 1 tsp ground cumin
- 1 tsp smoked paprika
- ½ to 1 tsp Aleppo red pepper flakes, plus more
- ¼ cup fresh white breadcrumbs (optional)
- distilled water (optional)
- assorted crudités or wedges of pita bread

Directions:

1. Supply your smoker with wood pellets and follow the start-up procedure. Preheat the grill, with the lid closed, to 400° F.

2. Place the peppers skin side down on the grate and grill until the skins blister and the flesh softens, about 30 minutes. Transfer the peppers to a bowl and cover with plastic wrap. Let cool to room temperature. Remove the skins with a paring knife or your fingers. Coarsely chop or tear the peppers.

3. Place ¾ cup of walnuts in an aluminum foil roasting pan. Place the pan on the grate and toast for 10 to 15 minutes, stirring twice. Remove the pan from the grill and let the walnuts cool.

4. Place the peppers, onion, garlic, and walnuts in a food processor fitted with the chopping blade. Pulse several times. Add the olive oil, balsamic vinegar, honey, salt, cumin, paprika, and red pepper flakes. Process until the mixture is fairly smooth. Taste for seasoning, adding more salt or red pepper flakes (if desired). (If the mixture is too loose, add breadcrumbs until the texture is to your liking. If it's too thick, add olive oil or water 1 tablespoon at a time.)

5. Transfer the dip to a serving bowl. Use the back of a spoon to make a shallow depression in the center. Top with the remaining ¼ cup of walnuts and drizzle olive oil in the depression. Serve with crudités or pita bread.

Bacon Pork Pinwheels (kansas Lollipops)

Servings: 4-6

Cooking Time: 20 Minutes

Ingredients:

➤ 1 Whole Pork Loin, boneless

➤ To Taste salt and pepper

➤ To Taste Greek Seasoning

➤ 4 Slices bacon

➤ To Taste The Ultimate BBQ Sauce

Directions:

1. When ready to cook, start the smoker and set temperature to 500F. Preheat, lid closed, for 10 to 15 minutes.

2. Trim pork loin of any unwanted silver skin or fat. Using a sharp knife, cut pork loin length wise, into 4 long strips.

3. Lay pork flat, then season with salt, pepper and Cavender's Greek Seasoning.

4. Flip the pork strips over and layer bacon on unseasoned side. Begin tightly rolling the pork strips, with bacon being rolled up on the inside.

5. Secure a skewer all the way through each pork roll to secure it in place. Set the pork rolls down on grill and cook for 15 minutes.

6. Brush BBQ Sauce over the pork. Turn each skewer over, then coat the other side. Let pork cook for another 5-10 minutes, depending on thickness of your pork. Enjoy!

BEEF LAMB AND GAME RECIPES

Asian Steak Skewers

Servings: 6

Cooking Time: 80 Minutes

Ingredients:

- 1 1/2 lbs top sirloin steak
- 6 garlic cloves, minced
- 1 red onion
- 1/3 cup sugar
- 3/4 cup soy sauce
- 1 tbsp ground ginger
- 1/4 cup sesame oil
- 3 tbsp sesame seeds
- 1/4 cup vegetable oil
- Bamboo skewers

Directions:

1. Cut sirloin steak into cubes, about 1 inch.

2. Cut red onion into chunks similar in size to the sirloin steak cubes.

3. In a bowl, combine and whisk soy sauce, sesame oil, vegetable oil, minced garlic, sugar, ginger, and sesame seeds.

4. Add steak to sauce bowl and toss to coat until steak is covered in the sauce.

5. Marinate for at least 1 hour in a refrigerator (if you are in a rush it's ok to skip this part, but you'll sacrifice a little bit of flavor).

6. Preheat pellet grill to 350°F.

7. Thread marinated beef and red onion pieces onto bamboo skewers.

8. Grill the skewers, turning after about 4 minutes. Cook for 8 minutes total or until meat reaches your desired doneness.

Wagyu Corned Beef Hash

Servings: 8

Cooking Time: 360 Minutes

Ingredients:

- 2 1/2 Pound Wagyu Corned Beef Roast
- 2 red bell pepper, diced
- 1 green bell pepper, diced
- 2 Pound Southern Hash Brown
- 3 Cup shredded cheddar cheese
- 2 Tablespoon kosher salt
- 2 Tablespoon black pepper
- 7 eggs
- 1/2 Cup whole milk

Directions:

1. Corned Beef: Corned beef needs to be cooked at least one day prior to making the hash.

2. Supply your smoker with wood pellets and follow the start-up procedure. Preheat the grill, with the lid closed, to 275° F.

3. Rinse the corned beef and place on grill. Cook for 4 to 4.5 hours. Wrap in a double layer of heavy duty tin foil and put back on the grill. Grill: 275 °F

4. Cook meat until it reaches an internal temperature of 204 degrees F. This should take 2-3 more hours. Let vent for 2 hours and place in fridge. Refrigerate overnight. Grill: 275 °F Probe: 204 °F

5. Corned Beef Hash: Chop and cook the peppers in cast iron for 20 minutes.

6. When ready to cook, start the Traeger and set the temperature to 350 degrees F and preheat, lid closed, for 10 minutes. Grill: 350 °F

7. Cut the corned beef into bite-sized pieces. Combine the hash browns, corned beef, bell peppers, cheese, salt and pepper. Mix well and place in a 9x13 baking dish.

8. Mix eggs and milk in a separate bowl. Pour over the top of the hash brown mixture.

9. Cover with foil and set on the grill for a 1.5 hours. The internal temperature should reach 165 degrees F. Serve and enjoy! Grill: 350 °F Probe: 165 °F

The Boss Beef Burger

Servings: 10   Cooking Time: 85 Minutes

Ingredients:

- 4 Lbs Beef, Ground
- 1 Loaf Bread, Sourdough Round
- 1/2 Cup Butter
- Condiments (Ketchup, Mustard, Relish, Etc.)
- Lettuce
- 3 Cups Mushroom
- 3 Onion, Chopped
- Kansas City BBQ Sauce
- Mandarin Habanero Spice
- 1 Lbs Pork, Ground
- Red Onion, Chopped
- 1 Bag Shredded Cheddar Cheese
- Tomato, Sliced

Directions:

1. Supply your smoker with wood pellets and follow the start-up procedure. Preheat the grill, with the lid closed, to 300° F.

2. In a large bowl, mix together the ground beef, ground pork, eggs, barbecue sauce, and seasoning until combined. Do not over mix as this will cause the meat to be tough after cooking. Split the mixture into two equal parts.

3. Melt the butter in a pan over medium heat and sauté the onion mushrooms until golden.

4. In a cast iron pan, flatten one half of the meat mixture into the bottom, taking care to work meat slightly up the sides of the pan. Sprinkle in half of the bag of cheese. Pour in onion mixture and top with the rest of the cheese.

5. On a clean work surface, mold the second half of the meat mixture into a circle and cover the filling to complete the burger. Make sure that the top and bottom meat patties are secured together so that the filling cannot be seen.

6. Place the cast iron pan in the Grill for 1 hour - 1 hour 15 minutes, or until the internal temperature reaches 160°F. Crank up the to "HIGH" and open the flame broiler. Flip the burger out of the cast iron pan onto the grates and sear each side for 5 minutes, to get those beautiful grill marks.

7. To serve: You can make an enormous burger like we did, or you can cut it like a pie into slices to be served on regular hamburger buns with your desired condiments.

Sweet And Spicy Beef Sirloin Tip Roast

Servings: 8

Cooking Time: 120 Minutes

Ingredients:

➢ 3 Pound beef sirloin tip roast

➢ 2 Tablespoon Beef Rub

➢ 1/2 Cup 'Que BBQ Sauce

➢ 1/4 Cup chili sauce

Directions:

1. Season sirloin tip roast evenly with Traeger Beef Rub on all sides. Let roast rest at room temperature for 30 minutes.

2. Supply your smoker with wood pellets and follow the start-up procedure. Preheat the grill, with the lid closed, to 275° F.

3. Place the roast on the Traeger and cook for about 75 minutes or until the internal temperature reaches 130°F. Grill: 275 ˚F Probe: 130 ˚F

4. In a small bowl, combine Traeger 'Que and chili sauce. Once meat has reached 130°F, brush the roast with 1/4 cup of the bbq chili sauce.

5. Continue cooking until internal temperature reaches 140°F. Grill: 275 ˚F Probe: 140 ˚F

6. Remove from the grill and place on a cutting board then tent with foil. Let stand 10 minutes or until internal temperature reaches 145°F.

7. Slice roast across the grain into thin slices and brush each slice with remaining sauce. Serve, enjoy!

Roasted Prime Rib With Mustard And Herbs De Provence

Servings: 8

Cooking Time: 180 Minutes

Ingredients:

- 1 Whole 7-bone prime rib roast
- extra-virgin olive oil
- kosher salt
- coarse ground black pepper
- 2 Cup Dijon mustard
- 2 Cup herbs de Provence

Directions:

1. Note: this recipe requires an overnight marinade, plan ahead. A day before you are ready to cook, prep your prime rib. Trim any excess fat.

2. Coat the prime rib evenly with olive oil to allow the seasoning to adhere. Season all sides of the roast generously with salt and pepper. Next, coat all sides evenly with a layer of Dijon mustard, and season liberally with the herbs de Provence. Let sit in the refrigerator for up to 24 hours, uncovered.

3. Supply your smoker with wood pellets and follow the start-up procedure. Preheat the grill, with the lid closed, to 325° F.

4. Place the prime rib fat side up, directly on the grill grate or on a sheet tray, and roast for 3 to 3 ½ hours, or until the internal temperature reaches 110°F.

5. Pull the prime rib off the grill and allow to rest for one hour. The internal temperature will continue to rise as it rests, you are looking for a finished temp of 130°F for medium rare.

6. Carve the roast. First stand the prime rib upright, and using a sharp, thin-bladed carving knife, carve along the bones, following the curvature of the bones as closely as you can until you cut through the base. Next, slice the roast into even slices, about 1" thick. To carve the bones, stand it upright again and slice along the bones. Enjoy!

Bbq Brisket Breakfast Tacos

Servings: 6

Cooking Time: 30 Minutes

Ingredients:

- 4 Pound leftover beef brisket
- 1/2 Teaspoon extra-virgin olive oil
- 1 green bell pepper, diced
- 1 Yellow Bell Pepper, diced
- 10 eggs
- 1/2 Cup milk
- salt and pepper
- 2 Cup shredded cheddar cheese
- flour tortillas

Directions:

1. Supply your smoker with wood pellets and follow the start-up procedure. Preheat the grill, with the lid closed, to 375° F.

2. Place leftover brisket in a double layer of foil and warm in grill. Grill: 375 ℉

3. Coat the inside of a cast iron skillet with oil and preheat the skillet in the grill for 10 minutes. When skillet is hot, sauté diced peppers, stirring every few minutes until desired doneness.

4. While peppers are cooking, whisk together the eggs, milk, salt and pepper to taste. Add the beaten eggs to the skillet and scramble. Add cheese to the skillet when the eggs are almost done.

5. Remove eggs and heated brisket from grill. Serve eggs in a tortilla topped with brisket. Top with salsa or guacamole if desired. Enjoy!

Salt & Pepper Beer-braised Beef Ribs

Servings: 4

Cooking Time: 180 Minutes

Ingredients:

- 2 Rack meaty beef back ribs
- coarse kosher or sea salt
- freshly ground black pepper
- granulated garlic
- 1 1/2 Cup beer or beef stock
- 'Que BBQ Sauce

Directions:

1. If your butcher has not already done so, remove the thin papery membrane from the bone-side of the ribs by working the tip of a butter knife or a screwdriver underneath the membrane over a middle bone. Use paper towels to get a firm grip, then tear the membrane off.

2. About an hour before cooking, put the ribs in a foil pan, meat-side up, and season the ribs on both sides with the salt, pepper and granulated garlic.

3. Supply your smoker with wood pellets and follow the start-up procedure. Preheat the grill, with the lid closed, to 165° F.

4. Arrange the pan of ribs on the grill grate and smoke for 1 hour. Pour the beer into the bottom of the pan (be careful not to wash the seasonings off the ribs). Cover the pan tightly with foil. Grill: 165 ˚F

5. Increase Traeger temperature to 250°F and continue to cook the ribs until the meat is meltingly tender, about 2 to 3 hours more. Grill: 250 ˚F

6. Carefully remove the foil. Discard the braising liquid and serve the ribs with Traeger 'Que BBQ Sauce. (You can brush the sauce on the ribs and sizzle them on the grill, or you can serve the sauce on the side.) Enjoy!

Cucumber Beef Kefta

Servings: 4

Cooking Time: 10 Minutes

Ingredients:

- bamboo skewers, soaked in warm water
- 1 tbsp blackened saskatchewan rub seasoning
- 3 tbsp cilantro, chopped
- for topping, cucumbers
- 1 tsp cumin
- 2 lbs ground beef
- 1 tsp paprika
- 3 tbsp parsley, chopped
- pitas
- 1 red onion, grated
- for topping, tomatoes
- to taste, tzatziki sauce

Directions:

1. In a mixing bowl, combine ground beef, onion, Blackened Saskatchewan, cumin, paprika, cilantro, and parsley. Mix well, then cover and refrigerate for 1 hour to allow the flavors to blend.

2. Supply your smoker with wood pellets and follow the start-up procedure. Preheat the grill, with the lid closed, to 425° F. If using a gas or charcoal grill, set it up for medium-high heat.

3. Prepare kebabs: take small amounts of ground beef kefta and shape into popsicle-size cylinders. Skewer the meat, squeezing it to mold it to the skewer.

4. Grill kefta 3 to 5 minutes per side, then remove from the grill and serve warm with pitas, tzatziki sauce, and your favorite fresh veggies.

Whiskey Bourbon Bbq Cheeseburger

Servings: 4

Cooking Time: 45 Minutes

Ingredients:

- 3 Pound ground beef
- Rub
- 1/2 Cup brown sugar
- 1 To Taste hot sauce
- 1/2 Cup bourbon whiskey
- 1 Pound bacon
- 4 Slices cheddar cheese

Directions:

1. In a medium bowl, combine ground beef and Traeger Rub and mix well using caution not to overwork or allow the beef to get too warm.

2. Divide the ground beef in quarters and put each quarter in a 6" cake ring. Press down and form the beef into a patty.

3. With a skewer, poke about 40 holes about ¾" of the way through each patty. Spread brown sugar all over the top of the patties then drizzle with hot sauce. Pour whiskey over each burger, transfer to the fridge and let sit for about a half hour.

4. Supply your smoker with wood pellets and follow the start-up procedure. Preheat the grill, with the lid closed, to 225° F.

5. Remove burgers from the cake rings. When the grill is to temp, place bacon and burgers directly on the grill grate and cook until burgers internal temperature reaches 165 °F. In the last ten minutes of cooking, top with cheddar cheese to melt. Grill: 225 °F Probe: 165 °F

6. Remove burgers and bacon from the grill and build your burger to your liking. Enjoy!

Braised Short Ribs

Servings: 2-4

Cooking Time: 240 Minutes

Ingredients:

➢ 4 beef short ribs

➢ Salt

➢ Freshly ground black pepper

➢ ½ cup beef broth

Directions:

1. Supply your smoker with wood pellets and follow the start-up procedure. Preheat the grill, with the lid closed, to 180°F.

2. Season the ribs on both sides with salt and pepper.

3. Place the ribs directly on the grill grate and smoke for 3 hours.

4. Pull the ribs from the grill and place them on enough aluminum foil to wrap them completely.

5. Increase the grill's temperature to 375°F.

6. Fold in three sides of the foil around the ribs and add the beef broth. Fold in the last side, completely enclosing the ribs and liquid. Return the wrapped ribs to the grill and cook for 45 minutes more. Remove the short ribs from the grill, unwrap them, and serve immediately.

Traeger Bacon-wrapped Filet Mignon

Servings: 2

Cooking Time: 15 Minutes

Ingredients:

- 3 (6 oz) filet mignon steaks
- 1 Teaspoon pepper
- 1 Teaspoon salt
- 2 Clove garlic, minced
- 3 Tablespoon butter, softened
- 3 Slices bacon

Directions:

1. Filets don't have much marbling, so when selecting meat look for a rich red color.

2. In a small bowl, combine salt, pepper, garlic and softened butter. Rub on both sides of filet. Let rest 10 minutes.

3. Supply your smoker with wood pellets and follow the start-up procedure. Preheat the grill, with the lid closed, to 450° F.

4. Wrap each steak in a slice of bacon and secure with a toothpick.

5. Place steaks directly on the grill and cook for 5 to 8 minutes on each side, or until the filets reach an internal temperature of 130℉ for medium-rare. Enjoy! Grill: 450 ℉ Probe: 130 ℉

K.i.s.s Texas Bbq Style Brisket

Servings: 8

Cooking Time: 240 Minutes

Ingredients:

- ➢ 1 1/2 Tablespoon coarse kosher or sea salt
- ➢ 1 1/2 Tablespoon medium grind black pepper
- ➢ 2 Teaspoon chili powder
- ➢ 1 (6 lb) flat cut brisket, trimmed
- ➢ 2 Cup beer, preferably Lone Star or other Texas beer
- ➢ 1/4 Cup bacon grease, lard or melted butter
- ➢ 2 Tablespoon Worcestershire sauce
- ➢ 1 Tablespoon garlic salt
- ➢ 1 Teaspoon red pepper flakes

Directions:

1. Supply your smoker with wood pellets and follow the start-up procedure. Preheat the grill, with the lid closed, to 225° F.

2. Combine rub ingredients in a small bowl and stir to mix. Season the brisket generously on both sides.

3. Put a wire cooling rack in a rimmed baking sheet or other shallow pan, then place the brisket, fat-side up, on the cooling rack. Place pan and brisket on the grill grate. Grill: 225 °F

4. Combine all the ingredients for the mop sauce in a nonreactive saucepan over medium heat. Bring to a simmer and stir until the salt dissolves. Re-warm before mopping the brisket so the fat (bacon grease, lard or butter) liquefies.

5. After the first hour, mop the brisket with the mop sauce; continue to mop every hour for the first 4 hours.

6. When the internal temperature of the meat reaches 165°F, wrap the meat tightly in butcher paper. (Note: Butcher paper is more permeable, but if you don't have access to any, use foil.) Grill: 225 °F Probe: 165 °F

7. Return the meat to the grill and continue to cook until the internal temperature reaches 203°F. (Total cooking time will vary, but plan on 6 to 8 hours total.) Grill: 225 °F Probe: 203 °F

8. Transfer the wrapped meat to an insulated cooler thickly lined with newspapers or bath towels.

9. Let the meat rest for at least 30 minutes. Reserve any juices that have accumulated in the baking sheet.

10. Unwrap the brisket. Thinly slice across the grain using an electric knife or sharp carving knife. Shingle the slices of brisket on a platter and pour the pan juices on top. Enjoy!

COCKTAILS RECIPES

Smoked Hibiscus Sparkler

Servings: 4

Cooking Time: 30 Minutes

Ingredients:

- 1/2 Cup sugar
- 2 Tablespoon dried hibiscus flowers
- 1 Bottle sparkling wine
- crystallized ginger, for garnish

Directions:

1. Supply your smoker with wood pellets and follow the start-up procedure. Preheat the grill, with the lid closed, to 180° F.

2. Place water in a shallow baking dish and place directly on the grill grate. Smoke the water for 30 minutes or until desired smoke flavor is achieved. Grill: 180 °F

3. Pour water into a small saucepan and add sugar and hibiscus flowers. Bring to a simmer over medium heat and cook until sugar is dissolved.

4. Strain out the hibiscus flowers and transfer your simple syrup to a small container and refrigerate until chilled.

5. Pour 1/2 ounce smoked hibiscus simple syrup in the bottom of a champagne glass and top with sparkling wine.

6. Drop in a few pieces of crystallized ginger to garnish. Enjoy!

Traeger Boulevardier Cocktail

Servings: 2

Cooking Time: 60 Minutes

Ingredients:

- 4 oranges
- 1/2 Cup honey
- 1500 mL rye whiskey
- 1 1/2 Ounce Campari
- 1 1/2 Ounce sweet vermouth
- 2 Tablespoon granulated sugar
- 3 Ounce grilled orange infused rye

Directions:

1. Supply your smoker with wood pellets and follow the start-up procedure. Preheat the grill, with the lid closed, to 350° F.

2. Slice 2 oranges in half and coat cut side with honey. Peel remaining orange and place peels on the grill. Cook 20 to 25 minutes. Grill: 350 ˚F

3. Remove from grill and let cool. Place orange halves cut side down directly on the grill grate and cook 20 to 30 minutes or until dark grill marks appear. Remove orange halves and allow to cool. Grill: 350 ˚F

4. Place orange halves into a bottle of rye whiskey and let steep for 10 to 12 hours. The longer they steep, the sweeter and more pronounced the orange flavor will be.

5. Add all ingredients into a mixing glass and stir until diluted. Strain into a fresh coupe glass and serve neat.

6. Garnish with grilled orange peel. Enjoy!

In Traeger Fashion Cocktail

Servings: 2

Cooking Time: 20 Minutes

Ingredients:

- ➢ 2 Whole orange peel
- ➢ 2 Whole lemon peel
- ➢ 3 Ounce bourbon
- ➢ 1 Ounce Smoked Simple Syrup
- ➢ 6 Dash Bitters Lab Charred Cedar & Currant Bitters

Directions:

1. Supply your smoker with wood pellets and follow the start-up procedure. Preheat the grill, with the lid closed, to 350° F.

2. Place the lemon and orange peel directly on the grill grate and cook 20 to 25 minutes or until lightly browned. Grill: 350 ˚F

3. Add bourbon, Traeger Smoked Simple Syrup and bitters to a mixing glass and stir over ice. Stir until glass is chilled and contents are well diluted.

4. Strain into a new glass over fresh ice and garnish with grilled lemon and orange peel. Enjoy!

Smoked Hot Buttered Rum

Servings: 4

Cooking Time: 30 Minutes

Ingredients:

- 2 Cup water
- 1/4 Cup brown sugar
- 1/2 Stick butter, melted
- 1 Teaspoon ground cinnamon
- 1/4 Teaspoon ground nutmeg
- ground cloves
- salt
- 6 Ounce Rum

Directions:

1. Supply your smoker with wood pellets and follow the start-up procedure. Preheat the grill, with the lid closed, to 180° F.

2. In a shallow baking dish, combine 2 cups water with all ingredients except for the rum and place directly on the grill grate. Smoke for 30 minutes. Grill: 180 ℉

3. Remove from the grill and pour into the pitcher of a blender. Process until somewhat frothy.

4. Pour 1.5 ounces of rum each into 4 glasses. Split hot butter mixture evenly between the four glasses.

5. Garnish with a cinnamon stick and freshly grated nutmeg. Enjoy!

Smoked Eggnog

Servings: 4

Cooking Time: 60 Minutes

Ingredients:

- 2 Cup whole milk
- 1 Cup heavy cream
- 4 egg yolk
- Cup sugar
- 3 Ounce bourbon
- 1 Teaspoon vanilla extract
- 1 Teaspoon nutmeg
- 4 egg white
- whipped cream

Directions:

1. Plan ahead, this recipe requires chill time.

2. Supply your smoker with wood pellets and follow the start-up procedure. Preheat the grill, with the lid closed, to 180˚ F.

3. Pour the milk and the cream into a baking pan and smoke on the Traeger for 60 minutes. Grill: 180 ˚F

4. Meanwhile, in the bowl of a stand mixer, beat the egg yolks until they lighten in color. Gradually add 1/3 cup sugar and continue to beat until sugar completely dissolves.

5. After the milk and cream have smoked, add them along with the bourbon, vanilla and nutmeg into the egg mixture and stir to combine.

6. Place the egg whites in the bowl of a stand mixer and beat to soft peaks. When you lift the beaters the whites will make a peak that slightly curls down.

7. With the mixer still running, gradually add 1 tablespoon of sugar and beat until stiff peaks form.

8. Gently fold the egg whites into the cream mixture and then whisk to thoroughly combine.

9. Chill eggnog for a couple hours to let the flavors meld. Garnish with a dash of nutmeg and whipped cream on top. Enjoy!

Traeger Gin & Tonic

Servings: 2

Cooking Time: 45 Minutes

Ingredients:

- 1/2 Cup berries
- 2 orange, sliced
- 4 Tablespoon granulated sugar
- 3 Ounce gin
- 1 Cup tonic water
- 2 Sprig fresh mint, for garnish

Directions:

1. Supply your smoker with wood pellets and follow the start-up procedure. Preheat the grill, with the lid closed, to 180° F.

2. For the Smoked Berries: Spread mixed fresh berries on a sheet pan and place directly on the grill grate. Smoke for 30 minutes then remove from grill. Grill: 180 °F

3. For the Orange Slices: Increase the grill temperature to 450°F and preheat, lid closed for 15 minutes. Grill: 450 °F

4. Toss the orange slices with granulated sugar and place directly on grill grate. Cook for about 5 minutes, turning once or until the slices have developed grill marks. Grill: 450 °F

5. Pour gin into a glass, add ice and berries, then top with tonic water. Garnish with a fresh mint sprig and grilled orange wheel. Enjoy!

Smoked Cold Brew Coffee

Servings: 8

Cooking Time: 120 Minutes

Ingredients:

➢ 12 Ounce coarse ground coffee

➢ heavy cream or milk

➢ sugar

Directions:

1. Place half the coffee grounds in a plastic container and slowly pour 3-1/2 cups water over the top of the grounds. Add remaining grounds and pour another 3-1/2 cups water over the top in a circular motion.

2. Press the grounds down into the water using the back of a spoon. Cover and transfer to the refrigerator and let sit for 18 to 24 hours.

3. Remove from refrigerator and strain into a clean container through a fine mesh strainer or double layer of cheese cloth.

4. Supply your smoker with wood pellets and follow the start-up procedure. Preheat the grill, with the lid closed, to 180° F.

5. Pour cold brew into a shallow baking dish and place directly on the grill grate. Smoke for 1 to 2 hours depending on desired level of smoke. Grill: 180 ˚F

6. Remove from grill and place over an ice bath to cool. Drink as is over ice, with cream or sugar or use in your favorite coffee recipes. Enjoy!

Grilled Rabbit Tail Cocktail

Servings: 2

Cooking Time: 25 Minutes

Ingredients:

- 1 1/2 Ounce lemon juice
- 4 Ounce Apple Brandy
- 1 Ounce orange juice
- 1 Ounce Smoked Simple Syrup

Directions:

1. Supply your smoker with wood pellets and follow the start-up procedure. Preheat the grill, with the lid closed, to 350° F.

2. Place lemon halves directly on the grill grate and cook for 20-25 minutes or until grill marks appear. Remove from grill and let cool. Once cool enough to handle, juice the lemons then chill and reserve the juice. Grill: 350 ℉

3. Using the proportions listed above and considering the size and consumption rate of your tailgate crew or party, mix all the above ingredients in a large thermos and top with a bit of ice.

4. Using 6-8 oz glasses or cups, guests can serve themselves from the thermos and garnish each drink with a grilled apple slice. Enjoy!

Strawberry Mule Cocktail

Servings: 2

Cooking Time: 15 Minutes

Ingredients:

- ➢ 8 grilled strawberries, plus more for serving
- ➢ 3 Ounce vodka
- ➢ 1 Ounce Smoked Simple Syrup
- ➢ 1 Ounce lemon juice
- ➢ 6 Ounce ginger beer
- ➢ fresh mint leaves

Directions:

1. Supply your smoker with wood pellets and follow the start-up procedure. Preheat the grill, with the lid closed, to 400° F.

2. Place strawberries directly on the grill grate and cook 15 minutes or until grill marks appear. Grill: 400 °F

3. For the cocktail: Add vodka, grilled strawberries, Traeger Smoked Simple Syrup and lemon juice to a shaker. Shake vigorously.

4. Double strain into a fresh glass or copper mug with crushed ice.

5. Top with ginger beer and garnish with extra grilled strawberries and fresh mint. Enjoy!

Printed by Libri Plureos GmbH in Hamburg,
Germany